THE REASON WHY

BASED ON THE CLASSIC BESTSELLER BY ROBERT A. LAIDLAW

THE REASON WHY

FAITH MAKES SENSE

MARK MITTELBERG

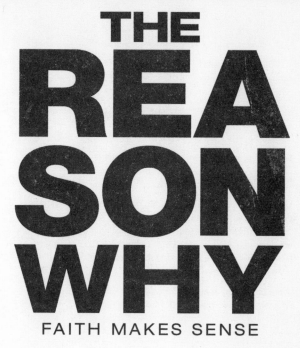

Tyndale House Publishers, Inc.
Carol Stream, Illinois

Visit Tyndale's exciting website at www.tyndale.com.

TYNDALE and Tyndale's quill logo are registered trademarks of Tyndale House Publishers, Inc.

The Reason Why

Copyright © 2011 by Mark Mittelberg. All rights reserved.

Designed by Mark Anthony Lane II

Published in association with the literary agency of Alive Communications, Inc., 7680 Goddard Street, Suite 200, Colorado Springs, CO 80920, www.alivecommunications.com.

Library of Congress Cataloging-in-Publication Data

Mittelberg, Mark.
   The reason why : faith makes sense / Mark Mittelberg.
      p. cm.
   Includes bibliographical references (p.   ).
   ISBN 978-1-4143-1581-2 (pbk.)
   1. Apologetics. I. Title.
   BT1103.M581934 2011
   239—dc22   2011000629

978-1-4143-1581-2
Printed in the United States of America

16   15   14   13   12
 7   6

To the memory of Robert A. Laidlaw,
businessman, Christian leader,
and author of the original book
The Reason Why,
which impacted the lives
of countless people
all over the world.

Contents

Foreword   *ix*

Introduction   *xiii*

Matters of Faith Really Matter   *1*

Is There a God?   *7*

Can the Bible Be Trusted?   *33*

Are We Accountable to God?   *47*

Who Was Jesus and What Was His
    Purpose?   *59*

Is Divine Forgiveness Available?   *73*

What Do I Need to Do?   *101*

My Decision   *121*

Next Steps   *123*

Postscript: The Soldier's Choice   *125*

Notes   *129*

Foreword

IN MANY WAYS I'm a latecomer to the Lord. Early in our marriage my wife, Margie, and I became so upset with the behavior of people in churches that we turned our back on God. Our first teaching job was at Ohio University in the mid-1960s during the height of the Vietnam War. A pastor friend of ours was leading the sit-ins protesting the war and his southeastern Ohio congregation fired him in the most vicious scandal we had ever seen.

To be honest, we didn't start thinking about God again until 1982, when *The One Minute Manager* came out. It was so ridiculously successful that I was having trouble taking credit for it. When people started asking me why I thought the book was so successful, I began saying, "Somehow God must be involved."

The minute I opened myself to God, He started sending incredible people into my life. For example, there was an eighty-six-year-old pastor who had a tremendous impact on Margie and me. He told us, "The Lord's always had you on His team—you just haven't suited up yet." I was the first one to "suit up"; Margie didn't join the faith at the same time. After all, turning your life over to the Lord is not a team activity.

She turned the corner on a snowy afternoon in Aspen, Colorado. Margie had hurt her knee and wasn't able to ski that day. Our longtime friend Phil Hodges (who would later become the cofounder of our Lead Like Jesus ministry) had fallen in love with the book Robert A. Laidlaw had written so many years ago, *The Reason Why*. Thinking it would be perfect for Margie, he asked her if she had time that day to read it.

When I returned from skiing that afternoon and walked into our bedroom, Margie was sitting there with a smile on her face.

She said, "Well, I suited up."

I said, "You did what?"

She said, "I read *The Reason Why* and when

Laidlaw asked for the declaration at the end of the book, I couldn't refute his arguments."

Margie was the president of our company; since Laidlaw was a successful businessman, he spoke her language. When I read it, I had a big "ah-ha" too. Laidlaw knew how to explain profound spiritual truths using helpful stories and illustrations that anyone could learn from. The only problem was that he wrote his book nearly a century ago, and over time much of his language and even some of his examples became dated and increasingly difficult for people in today's culture to access.

Thankfully, Mark Mittelberg has now recreated this book by giving it contemporary expressions, updated examples, additional information and evidence to back it all up—while retaining the practical tone and clarity as well as many of the pearls of wisdom from the original work.

Books on faith-related topics are everywhere. Some are heady and hard to understand. Others are simple, bordering on simplistic. Mittelberg's *The Reason Why* is neither; it speaks in down-to-earth yet intelligent terms, using everyday language and examples that all of us can grasp and gain from.

I highly recommend this remake of a classic and urge you to read it with an open mind and a receptive heart—seeking all that the Lord has for your own life and eternity.

Ken Blanchard
Coauthor of *The One Minute Manager* and *Lead Like Jesus*

Introduction

"Spiritual vertigo"—that's what a friend of mine calls it. It's that dizzying feeling you get when you suddenly sense that the arguments or claims you're hearing have knocked you off your spiritual moorings, leaving you wondering what you can really believe in and how you can be sure. If you haven't felt the doubts and anxiety associated with spiritual vertigo yet, you probably will—regardless of what you believe.

Our culture is bent on the idea of questioning everything, including whatever it is you're currently trusting in. The process of examining your beliefs can be very unsettling. On the other hand, it can force you to refine your assumptions and beliefs in order to make sure you know where they are pointed and why.

This happened to me years ago, when I took my Introduction to Philosophy class in college. I felt like I was in way over my head. As a business major, I wasn't sure I should even be *trying* to interact with what seemed at the time to be such lofty and out-of-reach ideas about knowledge, truth, "metaphysics," and faith.

Then one day our professor stood in front of our class and systematically challenged what he called the traditional view of God. He proclaimed that the concept of an eternal, unchanging, all-powerful God was based on ideas from a book—the Bible—that was written by hopelessly flawed human beings, had been edited and embellished over time, and was full of factual errors and contradictions.

If that's a view you hold, keep reading. But although things might be different today, at that time most of the students in class had grown up with the "traditional view," including me. I wanted to refute what the professor was saying, but the thought of getting up and challenging this learned teacher made my knees grow weak and mouth go dry. Worse yet, I realized I didn't really know what to say. I didn't agree with him, but I didn't know how to refute his claims. I felt intimidated and spiritually insecure.

What bothered me most as I left class that day was the realization that I hadn't ever thought deeply about many of the beliefs I'd grown up with. I'd accepted most of them by simple trust, expecting that my parents and teachers had told me the truth. But now I needed to know, in real terms, whether it made sense to hold on to my beliefs about God, Jesus, the Bible, and the message of divine grace and forgiveness. I wasn't anxious to throw away what I'd been taught, but I didn't want to take it all on faith, either. In short, I needed—and maybe you need—to find out whether there is a real basis for believing any of these things. Put another way, I needed to know *the reason why.*

You may have grown up with a background similar to mine. Or you may have been taught to hold very different religious views, or none at all. You might be reading this and realizing that you, too, have accepted most of your beliefs by simple trust, expecting that your parents and teachers have told you the truth without considering the claims seriously for yourself. But no matter what we grew up thinking about existential questions, the truth is that we all believe *something*. And as I did back in Intro to Philosophy, at some point we must each face the same issues: Is there meaning to life? Does faith make sense? Can logic or evidence point me toward a trustworthy set of beliefs? If so, which one?

• • •

The universal need for answers to these kinds of questions prompted Robert A. Laidlaw, an innovative and highly successful businessman in New Zealand, to write a powerful little book called *The Reason Why* a century ago. What he produced quickly mushroomed into a world-wide phenomenon.

Laidlaw initially wrote *The Reason Why* to explain his faith to his employees at the department store he founded in Auckland, Farmers Trading Company—a business that is still thriving today.[1] Initially he printed only 5,000 copies, thinking such a large quantity would probably last a lifetime. But there was such strong interest in the book that he had to immediately reprint it, and this process was repeated over and over again. Since that first edition it has been published in numerous forms and translated into more than thirty languages, and there are now more than 50 million copies in print![2]

I was first exposed to Laidlaw's book around the time I was feeling spiritual vertigo in that philosophy class. I found its information and anecdotes to be extremely down-to-earth and helpful. I read it through several times, as well as studying a number of other books that went into greater depth on the questions that most concerned me. This served to dramatically reinforce my faith. The irony is that after that rocky foray into the field of philosophy, and after completing my bachelor's degree in business management, I ended up earning my master's degree in philosophy of religion—and I have been speaking and writing in this area ever since.

But I keep going back to the simple brilliance of *The Reason Why*, and as a result I have given away literally hundreds of copies to people with all kinds of faith-related questions. I've found that its stories still pack a punch, but over the years I have increasingly realized that its language and some of its examples needed an update—and that its repertoire of reasons needed an expansion to address more of the issues being asked in our current culture. It was out of that awareness that the vision grew to write a new and expanded version of *The Reason Why* for a new generation.

With inspiration and some of the stories drawn from the original—mixed with many of my own approaches and examples—this is my humble attempt to present to my contemporaries the same important truths that Robert Laidlaw so effectively presented to his.

It is my sincere hope that what you read on the pages that follow will provide you with the reasons you need in order to find a clear and confident faith. Please read it with an open heart and a receptive mind. And as you proceed, be mindful of the promise Jesus made in Luke 11:9-10:

And so I tell you, keep on asking, and you will receive what you ask for. Keep on seeking, and you will find. Keep on

*knocking, and the door will be opened
to you. For everyone who asks, receives.
Everyone who seeks, finds. And to everyone
who knocks, the door will be opened.*

Mark Mittelberg
Denver, Colorado

Matters of Faith Really Matter

MAYBE YOU REALLY *will* live to the ripe old age of eighty, ninety, or even higher. Actuary tables say that these days your chances are fairly good. By most standards that would be a pretty long life span.

But have you ever thought of that length of time against the backdrop of eternity? Try plotting those eighty years on a chart next to eternity and you'll soon realize that your entire earthly life is represented by a tiny dot that's barely visible next to what follows it! What if all your days here are mostly just preparation for the life that comes next—the *real* one? How would knowing that now affect your priorities and daily decisions?

Let's look at this from another angle. Suppose

a young man sends his fiancée a beautiful diamond ring that costs him $15,000, putting it in the little case that the jeweler throws in for free. Just imagine how shocked he would be if she responded by saying, "Thank you, sweetheart—that was such a nice little box you sent me! To take special care of it, I promise to keep it wrapped up in a safe place so nothing will ever happen to it."

That seems ridiculous, doesn't it? Yet isn't it just as foolish for people like us to spend all our time and energy on our bodies, which are only containers of our real self, the soul, which, according to Jesus and the writers of the Bible, will persist long after our bodies have turned to dust?[1] When you think of it that way, it's easy to see that the soul has immeasurable value.

In fact, Jesus—known for his ability to speak directly to the heart of a matter—asked in Mark 8:36-37: "And what do you benefit if you gain the whole world but lose your own soul? Is anything worth more than your soul?" Our response to his question today is the same as it was when he first posed it: awkward silence, because the obvious answer is, "No, nothing!"

A person's soul—my soul or your soul—according to Jesus, is incomparably more valuable than the entire world of possessions, pleasures, power, and prestige.

Maybe you aren't so sure about matters of the soul at this point in your life. Perhaps the whole realm of the spiritual seems unreal or unimportant to you, or like something you'd rather not think about until later—like when you get closer to that seemingly distant age of eighty or ninety.

Staying Open

May I encourage you to think again, and at least to say, "Maybe"? Admit to yourself that if these things are true, then Jesus' point about the importance of the soul is valid—*big time*! Do you doubt that? Then at least be consistent enough as a skeptic to also doubt even your own doubts—and keep reading. As you turn the pages, keep saying to yourself, "Maybe God *is* real"; "Maybe the Bible *is* God's message to us"; "Maybe Jesus truly *was* the Son of God"; "Maybe I *need* what Jesus offers me"; "Maybe

God is speaking to *me*." I'm not asking you to take any blind leaps of faith, just to be open-minded enough to genuinely consider the possibility that these things could be true.

Could I also suggest that you offer a can't-miss prayer? You may not be comfortable with prayer, so move on if you need to. But you don't have to try to sound religious to pray. You can just sincerely say something like this, whether silently or out loud:

> *God, if you're there and if these things I'm reading are really true, please show me. If you'll make it clear to me, then I promise to respond to you accordingly. Amen.*

God loves answering straightforward prayers like that! A man once came to Jesus, having enough faith to ask him for a miracle—but enough doubt to second-guess whether his request would really do any good. Jesus said to him, "Anything is possible if a person believes." The man responded with wonderful transparency: *"I do believe, but help me overcome my unbelief!"* And guess what? Jesus honored that sincere doubter's prayer, performing the miracle for him right then and there.[2]

So be honest about your spiritual perspective—but also active in your pursuit of truth and answers for your life. I'm confident God will meet you somewhere in the middle.

Key Faith Issues

Let's talk about some of the central questions that relate to the part of us that Jesus called our most valuable possession, our souls. I think it will quickly become clear that these matters really do matter—not just for some future life in the hereafter, but for the nitty-gritty realities of daily living, as well. These include the following:

Is there a God?

Can the Bible be trusted?

Are we accountable to God?

Who was Jesus and what was his purpose?

Is divine forgiveness available?

What do I need to do?

These are some of the questions that most perplex those who think seriously about spiritual matters, their own lives, and their future.

IS THERE A GOD?

WHILE THE VAST majority of people believe in God or some form of divine being, it has become fashionable to deny God's existence and to declare oneself an atheist. Just scan the shelves of many bookstores—especially, and ironically, the *religion* sections. Many of the top sellers are actually anti-God books written by spiritual skeptics. Or surf the Internet and you'll see that, increasingly, the boldest and brashest opinions are being presented by people who decry the idea of God altogether.

Why is that? Has there been some new discovery that disproves the existence of a deity? Have the claims of the supernatural been conclusively refuted to the point that we can now deduce that there is no God?

To the contrary, the evidence *for* God is growing day by day as thinking people—including scientists, historians, archeologists, philosophers, and others, many of whom were former skeptics—find more and more support for the existence of God and for the claims of Christianity in particular. In fact, the strength of the evidence is mounting to the extent that one popular book came out recently with the title *I Don't Have Enough Faith to Be an Atheist.*[1]

I like that title because it really does seem to me that the problems of unbelief in God are greater than the problems of belief. To accept that nothing produced everything, nonlife produced life, randomness produced order, chaos produced information, unconsciousness produced consciousness, and non-reason produced reason would require a lot more faith than I'd be able to muster!

Why then the continual onslaught of skeptical literature and opinion? There are probably a variety of reasons—many of which have little or nothing to do with reason. But if you look at the ideas being furthered and the rationale that often goes with them, you'll find that many people have simply decided— from the outset and apart from compelling evidence or real interaction with the actual arguments for God—that belief in a divine being is unthinkable, so they don't even give it serious thought.

This approach betrays what is sometimes called an "anti-supernatural bias." In other words, the person has decided in advance that there is nothing in our world beyond nature and then proceeds to dismiss or attack any opinions to the contrary. By way of example, back in the 1940s critical theologian Rudolf Bultmann declared, "It is impossible to use electric light and the wireless and to avail ourselves of modern medical and surgical discoveries, and at the same time to believe in the New Testament world of spirits and miracles."[2]

This opinion has only intensified in our current age of discovery—and skepticism. For example, the radical left-leaning "Jesus Seminar" scholars published a book that claimed, "The Christ of creed and dogma, who had been firmly in place in the Middle

Ages, can no longer command the assent of those who have seen the heavens through Galileo's telescope. The old deities and demons were swept from the skies by that remarkable glass."[3]

That's quite a claim! But pronouncing something is not the same as proving it. In fact, upon analysis, these opinions assume the very thing they purport to prove. This is the age-old fallacy of circular reasoning. They are saying, in effect, "Modern people can no longer believe in the supernatural because . . . well . . . they're modern people!"

Now, I'm all for electric lights, using a "wireless" (especially the kind we have *today*), enjoying the benefits of modern medicine, and learning all we can through the latest telescopes—but none of that even begins to address the growing body of evidence we have for God's existence. The question we need to ask is not whether we are technologically advanced, but what is the evidence for God—and how will we respond to it? In the next section we'll look at several lines of compelling evidence.[4]

Reasons for Believing in God

Evidence from the Beginning of the Universe

Every thoughtful person believes in a series of causes and effects in nature, each effect becoming the cause of some other effect. This is the basis of all scientific inquiry. Albert Einstein put it like this: "The scientist is possessed by the sense of universal causation."[5] But the acceptance of this as fact compels one to admit that there must be a beginning to any series—or the chain of events never would have gotten started. There could never have been a first effect if there had not been a first cause.

Consider the logic that flows through these three statements:[6]

- Whatever has a beginning has a cause.
- The universe has a beginning.
- Therefore, the universe has a cause.

The first statement, *Whatever has a beginning has a cause*, can be illustrated with a couple of real-life scenarios. If you go to the doctor to find out why a lump has begun to grow in your throat, you're not going to be satisfied to hear there's no cause for the lump—that it just sprang up for no reason. If he or she tries to pass off an explanation like that, you're going to find a new doctor!

Or if you're a parent, and you go into one of your kids' rooms and find a hole punched through the wall, you're not going to accept a causeless, self-existent hole-in-the-wall theory. Instead, you want a real explanation from your son or daughter—the old-fashioned kind that actually explains what happened.

Just as the appearance of lumps in your throat or holes in your kids' walls needs an explanation, so does the sudden appearance of a universe!

The second statement says *The universe has a beginning.* The only other options are to say that it is eternal and has simply always been there— an answer akin to the causeless, self-existent hole-in-the-wall theory—or to claim that it popped into existence out of thin air. But as the song in the classic movie *The Sound of Music* so poignantly reminds us, "Nothing comes from nothing, nothing ever could."

Common sense tells us that the universe had a beginning, but we know this through modern science as well. Robert Jastrow, astronomer and founding director of NASA's Goddard Institute for Space Studies, summarized the conclusion of decades of scientific research in his powerful book *God and the Astronomers*:

> *Five independent lines of evidence—the motions of the galaxies, the discovery of the primordial fireball, the laws of thermodynamics, the abundance of helium in the Universe and the life story of the stars—point to one conclusion; all indicate that* the Universe had a beginning.[7]

Jastrow also goes into detail concerning what scientists believe about that amazing beginning, usually referred to in scientific circles as the Big Bang[8]:

> *The matter of the Universe is packed together into one dense mass under enormous pressure, and with temperatures ranging up to trillions of degrees. The*

*dazzling brilliance of the radiation in
this dense, hot Universe must have been
beyond description. The picture suggests
the explosion of a cosmic hydrogen bomb.
The instant in which the cosmic bomb
exploded marked the birth of the
Universe.*

*The seeds of everything that has
happened in the Universe since were
planted in that first instant; every star,
every planet and every living creature
in the Universe owes its physical origins
to events that were set in motion in the
moment of the cosmic explosion. In a
purely physical sense, it was the moment
of creation.*[9]

Popular theoretical physicist Stephen Hawking
adds these amazing details about the astounding rate of expansion of the universe resulting
immediately from the Big Bang, or what physicists refer to as "inflation":

*According to even conservative
estimates, during this cosmological*

inflation, the universe expanded by a factor of 1,000,000,000,000,000,000, 000,000,000,000 in .0000000000000 00000000000000000000001 second. It was as if a coin 1 centimeter in diameter suddenly blew up to ten million times the width of the Milky Way.[10]

Don't rush over that quote too quickly—it warrants a second and maybe a third reading. This is a highly regarded scientist telling us what virtually every modern scientist believes: that the universe expanded at a rate equivalent to a coin in your pocket becoming many millions of times wider than our entire galaxy—which all of the efforts of modern space exploration have barely even begun to explore—and it did this in a fraction of a nanosecond! But neither Hawking nor any physicist on earth has a scientific explanation for why or how that happened.

In theological terms, we call this a *miracle*.

So both logic and science tell us that the universe had a beginning—and a spectacularly grand one at that. And we established earlier that whatever has a beginning has a cause. So

this leads us to the natural conclusion of the
third statement listed previously: *The universe
had a cause.*

But that leads us to the realization that the
cause had to be something *outside the universe.*
And that "something" would have to be smart
enough, powerful enough, and old enough—
not to mention have enough of a creative, artis-
tic flair—to be able to pull off such a grand
"effect." That sounds to me like something
uncannily similar to the divine being described
in the Bible, which starts with these words: "In
the beginning God created the heavens and
the earth."[11] He's the same one of whom King
David wrote (Psalm 19:1-4):

> *The heavens proclaim the glory of God.*
> *The skies display his craftsmanship.*
> *Day after day they continue to speak;*
> *night after night they make him known.*
> *They speak without a sound or word;*
> *their voice is never heard.*
> *Yet their message has gone throughout*
> *the earth,*
> *and their words to all the world.*

Evidence from Design in the Universe

Suppose you are standing at an airport, watching a jet airliner coming in to land. Someone says to you, "A lot of people think that plane is the result of someone's carefully designed plans, but I know better. There was really no intelligence at work on it at all. In some strange way the metal just came out of the ground and fashioned itself into flat sheets. And then these metal sheets slowly began to grow together and formed the fuselage and wings and tail. Then after a long while the engines slowly grew in place, and one day some people came along and discovered the plane, all finished and ready to fly."

You would probably think that guy was crazy, and perhaps try to avoid him in the future. Why? You know intuitively that where there is a design, there must be a designer, and having seen other products of the human mind like the airplane, you are sure that it was planned by human intelligence and built by human skill.

Yet there are sophisticated and highly educated people who tell us that the entire universe, with all its order and intricate design, came into being by chance—that there was really no higher intelligence involved. They claim that there is no God but nature. The American astronomer and television personality Carl Sagan, for example, frequently told his TV viewers with great exuberance that "the Cosmos is all that is or was or ever will be."

More recently Stephen Hawking declared in his book *The Grand Design* that "spontaneous creation is the reason there is something rather than nothing, why the universe exists, why we exist. It is not necessary to invoke God."[12] Yet Hawking apparently cannot escape the principle that *design* points back to a *designer*—when only a few pages later, in the acknowledgments section, he says that "the universe has a design, and so does a book. But unlike the universe, a book does not appear spontaneously from nothing. A book requires a creator." That's quite a statement! Looking at his book—including the quote cited above about the mind-boggling expansion of matter at the Big Bang—I think it's safe to say that if *it* needed a designer, then the *universe* needs one countless times more.

This is true especially in light of our growing

understanding of what many thinkers, including renowned physicist Paul Davies, refer to as the "fine-tuning" of the universe.[13] Cutting-edge science is now telling us that the building blocks of our world—the laws and physical constants that govern all the matter in the universe—appear to be precisely balanced and finely tuned for life to occur and flourish.[14]

These laws and constants were set at the Big Bang mentioned earlier. In other words, when the universe exploded into being, there were a number of variables within the very structure of the universe itself that had to be set exactly as they are in order for life to exist. Scientists have so far discovered about *fifty* of these parameters and constants that must be "just so" in order for life to be possible anywhere in the universe.

Let's look at an example. Physicists have discovered four forces in nature, one of them being the force of gravity. They have calculated that the strength of each of these forces must fall within a very specific range or there would be no conscious life possible. If the force of gravity, for example, were to change by one part in ten thousand billion billion billion relative to the total range of the strengths of the four forces in nature, conscious life would be virtually impossible anywhere in the universe.[15]

There are many other parameters and constants that are also finely tuned and that, if changed even slightly, would have disastrous consequences for life in our universe. For example, if the neutron were not exactly as it is—about 1.001 times the mass of the proton—then all protons would have decayed into neutrons or all neutrons would have decayed into protons and life would not be possible. Or if the explosion of the Big Bang had differed in strength by as little as one part in 10^{60} (one part in a trillion trillion trillion trillion trillion), the universe would have either quickly collapsed back on itself or expanded too swiftly for stars to form. Either way, life would be impossible. The list of such fixed parameters goes on and on.[16]

What makes all this even more fascinating is that these finely tuned parameters and constants are independent of one another. In other words, assuming all were just right for life except for one parameter, which was off to the smallest degree, that alone would make it impossible for you or me to be alive today.

When you add this all up, it becomes virtually impossible to believe all of these fine-tuned constants came to be "just so" by chance. British astronomer Fred Hoyle started out as an atheist but eventually coined the term *big bang* derisively, famously saying, "A common sense interpretation of the facts suggests that a super-intellect has monkeyed with physics, as well as with chemistry and biology, and that there are no blind forces worth speaking about in nature." And if that weren't enough, he added, "The numbers one calculates from the facts seem to me so overwhelming as to put this conclusion almost beyond question."[17]

• • •

Think about *light* for a moment. What is it exactly? As simple as the question seems, it's actually a very challenging entity to understand. One definition is "the range of electromagnetic radiation that can be detected by the human eye." Does that clear things up? Scientists tell us that light is made up of waves. Or particles. Or both. But they're not completely sure how the two aspects of light—waves and particles—coexist and interact with each other.

If scientists are still trying to define and explain the nature of light, then why do we believe it exists at all? Because we see it—or perhaps more accurately, we see *with* it. Either way, we don't have to fully grasp what light is in order to believe in it and benefit from it. Similarly, although we can't fully define God, we can know that he exists because we see the manifestations of him everywhere around us.

Dr. Wernher von Braun, onetime director of NASA research and developer of the rocket that put America's first space satellite into orbit, said this:

In our modern world, many people seem to feel that our rapid advances in the field of science render such things as religious belief untimely or old-fashioned. They wonder why we should be satisfied in "believing" something when science tells us that we "know" so many things. The simple answer to this contention is that we are confronted with many more mysteries of nature today than when the age of scientific enlightenment began. With every new answer unfolded, science has consistently discovered at least three new questions.

The answers indicate that everything as well ordered and perfectly created as are our earth and universe must have a Maker, a Master Designer. Anything so orderly, so perfect, so precisely balanced, so majestic as this creation can only be the product of a Divine idea.[18]

Indeed, it was his observations of the amazing order and design of the universe as seen through his telescope that led astronomer Robert Jastrow, author of *God and the Astronomers*, to abandon his atheism and begin believing in God.

More recently Dr. Antony Flew, considered the world's greatest philosophical atheist and the author of the classic text *The Presumption of Atheism*, abandoned his atheism late in life. A few years before his death he wrote his final book, *There Is a God: How the World's Most Notorious Atheist Changed His Mind.*[19]

Lee Strobel and I had the opportunity to talk with Dr. Flew before he died. We asked him what caused him to reorient his thinking. Flew's response focused on one particular issue: "Einstein felt that there must be intelligence behind the integrated complexity of the physical world," he told us. "If that is a sound argument, the integrated complexity of the *organic* world is just inordinately greater—all the creatures are complicated pieces of design. So an argument that is important about the physical world is immeasurably stronger when applied to the biological world."[20]

Edwin Conklin, himself a noted biologist, would have concurred with these conclusions, as he expressed in his famous quote comparing the probability of life originating from accident to that of an unabridged dictionary resulting from an explosion in a printing shop.

Additional Lines of Evidence

Many other arguments can and have been given, including the amazing evidence of information that is encoded in DNA—a complex, cryptographic, four-letter code that is, as former president Bill Clinton once put it, "the language in which God created life."[21] Yet wherever we have language or information, we know there has to be an intelligence behind it. This powerfully points us to a *Divine Encoder*.

Then there is the evidence of morality throughout the human race. You see, each of us has an internal standard of morality—but one that is above us and comes from outside of us. Why do I say that the source of this morality is above and outside us? Because everybody has it, yet nobody consistently lives up to it. Why would we each invent a code of ethics that we could never quite fulfill, and then employ it to frustrate and condemn ourselves all life long? If morality were mere choice or convention, we could much more easily let go of it.

So where did we get this inescapable sense of right and wrong? If we didn't invent it, if it transcends the realms of culture and politics—which it clearly does—and if it's something we can't get away from, then what is its source? Could it be that a *Moral Lawgiver* actually knit those moral standards, along with the ability to understand and operate by them, into the very fabric of what it means to be human? That, it seems to me, is where the evidence clearly points.[22]

Beyond all of this, there is the historical evidence for Jesus and his exemplary life, his amazing fulfillment of numerous ancient prophecies, his many miracles done in broad daylight and in front of hostile witnesses (convincing a great number of them to follow him), his uncanny and seemingly supernatural insights into people's minds, and his astounding resurrection from the dead—well documented by many, including those who were not his followers—three days after his crucifixion. All of these realities point powerfully to the existence of a divine heavenly Father, as well as to the divinity of Jesus himself, who gave us countless reasons to believe he was truly God's Son.[23]

In addition to these varieties of evidence that point to the reality of God, I have an internal conviction that he exists. No matter how often I've doubted or tried to ignore him in the past, that "still, small voice" has come to me again and again, just as it comes to you—maybe even right now—in the quiet of life's more sober moments. Yes, I am confident that there is a God. And as I watch the lives of others, I realize that many of them are looking for God, seeking in "religion" to understand or perhaps to try to appease that same voice that is speaking within them.

Much more could be said, but the evidence for God is strong and getting stronger. It's important to add that God exists whether or not people choose to believe in him. Think about it: our belief in things does not affect whether they actually exist. We can imagine and meditate intently on the concept of unicorns, but that doesn't make one pop into existence. And the corollary to this is that our lack of belief in something that is real is not going to make it go away. If I have cancer, to give a negative example, I can try to deny it day and night, but that's not going to get rid of it.

The bottom line is this: *whatever is, is.* Our knowledge or trust in a thing's reality has no effect whatsoever on its existence. And if that's true in every other area of life, then why should we suppose it's any different when it comes to belief in God?

If the evidence is so great and so clear, why such reluctance to consider it? I think the reason many people do not acknowledge God is not so much that it is intellectually difficult to believe in him, but rather that belief in God forces a person to face the fact that he or she is accountable to him. Many people are unwilling to accept accountability to anyone, let alone God. Romans 1:18-19 says that they "know the truth about God because he has made it obvious to them," but that they "suppress the truth." That's why I think many take refuge in atheism or agnosticism—because it is a convenient escape from the challenging reality that they are accountable to their Creator. What is presented as "I cannot believe" is more usually in reality "I do not want to believe."

Outspoken atheist Jean-Paul Sartre, for example, described in his autobiography, *The Words*, what led him as a child to reject faith in God: "Only once did I have the feeling that He existed. I had been playing with matches and burned a small rug. I was in the process of covering up my crime when suddenly God saw me. I felt His gaze inside my head and on my hands. I whirled about in the bathroom, horribly visible, a live target. Indignation saved me. I flew into a rage against so crude an indiscretion, I blasphemed. . . . He never looked at me again. . . . I had all the more difficulty getting rid of [the Holy Ghost] in that he had installed himself at the back of my head. . . . I collared the Holy Ghost in the cellar and threw him out."[24]

Well-known author and atheist Aldous Huxley admitted, "I had motives for not wanting the world to have a meaning. . . . For myself, as, no doubt, for most of my contemporaries, the philosophy of meaninglessness was essentially an instrument of liberation. The liberation we desired was simultaneously liberation from a certain political and economic system and liberation from a certain system of morality. We objected to the morality because it interfered with our sexual freedom."[25]

And Christopher Hitchens, author of the best-selling diatribe *God Is Not Great: How Religion Poisons Everything*, describes himself not as an atheist, but as an "antitheist."[26] Well, I mentioned the idea of unicorns earlier; I don't believe in them, but I certainly would not describe myself as an "anti-unicornist." Such passion from atheists—and often anger, too—seems strange when aimed at something that, according to them, does not exist.

I think these examples, as well as the vitriol with which many skeptics attack God and his followers on the Internet, betray the fact that atheism is often motivated by personal or moral issues, not an actual weakness in the evidence for God.

• • •

Just as a good detective can tell you many things about my skills, habits, and character merely by examining something I have made or handled, much can be learned about God by a careful examination of the universe, the work of his hands.

But the detective who examines only what I make can never say he knows me. He may know some things *about* me, but before he can say he knows me there must be a process of revelation; in other words, I must communicate with him. I need to tell him what I think, how I feel, and what I want to do. This self-disclosure may be made in conversation, in writing, or in some other way. Only then does it become possible for him to really know me.

Likewise, if God is ever to be known and his thoughts, desires, and purposes understood, he must take the initiative and make at least a partial revelation of himself to the people he has created.

Has God done this? That's the question we will address next.

CAN THE BIBLE BE TRUSTED?

THE BIBLE IS the best-selling book of all time. A staggering 100 million copies are printed every year, and it is estimated that worldwide there are nearly 8 billion in print. The text of the Bible has been published in 450 different languages, the New Testament portion in 1,400 languages, and the Gospel of Mark in 2,370 languages. And these figures do not include the many digital versions of the Bible that millions of people view online.[1] Clearly this is a book that people are interested in—and their fascination only seems to keep growing.

The Bible is also a book that makes big claims and promises. It says it is a message from God—a revelation of the kind mentioned previously, telling us of himself and his purposes for us. And it declares that it has enduring value and relevance, as explained in Isaiah 40:8: "The grass withers and the flowers fade, but the word of our God stands forever."

It has been called an owner's manual for people—a book written through the inspiration of our Maker as a guide to help us live in a way that honors him and that works out for our own good as well. Second Timothy 3:16 explains, "All Scripture is . . . useful to teach us what is true and to make us realize what is wrong in our lives. It corrects us when we are wrong and teaches us to do what is right."

The problem is that there are a number of other religious books also claiming to be inspired by God. What sets the Bible apart, giving us confidence that it really is what it claims to be—God's revelation—and that it alone best "corrects us when we are wrong and teaches us to do what is right"? Much could be said in answer to that question, but here's a brief summary of some of the Bible's unique attributes:

- *Consistency.* Even though it was written over a span of one-and-a-half millennia by more than forty authors, in several different languages, and addressing hundreds of topics, it displays an uncanny uniformity in its message. This degree of consistency is hard enough to achieve within a single book by a lone author—but when you add the complexity of multiple writers, from multiple countries, in multiple languages, over multiple centuries, dealing with multiple problems and situations, the Bible's incredible cohesion and unified message are nothing short of astounding.

· *Historical Reliability.* The Old Testament record of God's activity in the world and among his people has been substantiated over and over by secular history and archaeological discoveries. The accounts in the Bible, and particularly those in the New Testament, are based primarily on direct, eyewitness testimony. As the apostle John wrote, "That which was from the beginning, which we have heard, which we have seen with our eyes, which we have looked at and our hands have touched—this we proclaim" (1 John 1:1, NIV). Other parts were compiled by writers who interacted with the actual eyewitnesses. This includes careful and conscientious historians like Luke, who made a point of explaining his research methodology at the beginning of his biography of Jesus: "Many people have set out to write accounts about the events that have been fulfilled among us. They used the eyewitness reports circulating among us from the early disciples. Having carefully investigated everything from the beginning, I also have decided to write a careful account . . . so you can be certain of the truth of everything you were taught" (Luke 1:1-4). In addition, the New Testament is confirmed at various points by early Jewish, Greek, and Roman historians, as well as second-generation disciples who affirmed its accuracy both in terms of authorship and content.

- *Textual Superiority.* The typical non-biblical ancient writing has a very small number of surviving manuscript copies, and most of those date to hundreds of years after the original document was written. A good example is Caesar's *Gallic Wars*, of which we have only ten surviving manuscript copies, the earliest dating a full 1,000 years after the original was written. Another is the writings of Tacitus, of which we have a total of about twenty full or partial copies, with a time gap between the original writings and the earliest copies of 1,100 years.[2] Yet these historical works are still considered to be essentially reliable. That being the case, when you consider that for the New Testament we have 5,700 manuscript or partial manuscript copies in Greek alone (and about 20,000 more in other languages), and the earliest fragment goes back to within a few decades of the original writing, you begin to understand that there is simply no comparison between it and other works of antiquity—and that the Bible we read today is an accurate copy of the original writings.

- *Archaeological Verifiability.* Literally thousands of details in the Bible, including references to specific people, places, and events, have been proved accurate through modern archaeological excavations and study. Sir William M. Ramsay of Oxford University, one of the great archaeologists of the last century, started out as a staunch skeptic, doubting many of the details recorded in the New Testament. Specifically, he thought Luke was foolish in his storytelling because he named so many specific names, locations, and dates. These specifics would be easy to check out and refute—assuming, as Ramsay did at the beginning, that they were not actually true. But over his thirty years of study, research, and excavation, Ramsay increasingly realized that Luke's writings in both the Gospel of Luke and the book of Acts were accurate records of the events and details they reported. He later summarized his findings in this way: "Luke is a historian of the first rank. . . . This author should be placed along with the very greatest of historians."[3] Also, renowned archaeologist Nelson Glueck, who was once featured on the cover of *Time* magazine because of his extraordinary work, concluded, "No archaeological discovery has ever controverted a single biblical reference."[4] No other "holy book" outside of the Bible has ever earned such overwhelming support and affirmation—or given us so many reasons to be confident in its integrity as we read.

• *Supernatural Activity.* The Bible gives powerful evidence that it was supernaturally inspired through numerous detailed prophecies that were recorded earlier and then fulfilled to the letter centuries later; through its record of miracles done by a number of Old Testament prophets as well as New Testament apostles—and especially by Jesus himself (including those performed in the presence of skeptics and opponents who never disputed their authenticity); and through its clear "ring of truth" that countless readers have affirmed over the centuries. They report that as they read the Bible, it speaks to the exact thing they're going through—making them feel like God is talking directly to them. It's an interesting observation, given that the Bible says in Hebrews 4:12, "For the word of God is alive and powerful. It is sharper than the sharpest two-edged sword, cutting between soul and spirit, between joint and marrow. It exposes our innermost thoughts and desires." Also, Jesus told us in John 10:27, "My sheep listen to my voice; I know them, and they follow me."

- *Spiritual Authority.* The truths written in the Bible, when accepted and lived out by ordinary people, have impacted millions of lives throughout the millennia— mine being one of them. In addition, almost all major advances in Western civilization have come about because people read, believed, and acted upon the Bible's message. Its positive influence is unrivaled in human history. Great social movements such as the abolition of slavery, civil rights, women's rights, sanctity of life, care for the poor, and the rule of law instead of dictatorial tyranny have been energized by those steeped in biblical teaching.

• • •

In spite of the Bible's being available to hundreds of millions of people, as well as the fact that its message has had an immeasurable impact on individuals and entire cultures in the past, there is a real problem.

"Americans revere the Bible," pollster George Gallup, Jr. observed, "but, by and large, they don't read it."[5] This is a tragedy—and one that is probably true of all nations, not just the United States. But let's not allow it to be true of you and me. The Bible is a book of such importance and influence that it is worthy of our thoughtful investigation. To be fair to ourselves and to the Bible, we should read it for ourselves, in a modern translation that is clear, accurate, and easy to understand.[6]

So in keeping with the classic advice "neither to accept nor reject, but to weigh and consider," let us consider this book and its extraordinary claims. You don't have to approach it as God's Word, but for what it at the minimum clearly is: an essentially reliable historical record.[7] Start by reading the four Gospels in the New Testament—Matthew, Mark, Luke, and John—which are early accounts of the life, ministry, and spiritual impact of Jesus Christ. Next, read the book of Acts to understand the amazing story of the beginnings and growth of the early Christian church. Then move on to Romans (especially chapters 1–8), which many believe to be the Bible's clearest presentation of the central message of the gospel. By that point you'll already be more than halfway through the New Testament, so keep reading until you complete it.

Just as a judge must not reach a conclusion when the information is half heard, neither must we. Rather, like good judges, we should hear the whole case, compare the testimonies of the witnesses, and weigh and consider each piece of evidence, seeking its deepest significance rather than accepting only its surface meaning.[8] Only in so doing can we reach a worthy verdict.

• • •

As I consider the evidence for the Bible, the truth of 2 Peter 1:20-21 becomes increasingly certain to me: "Above all, you must realize that no prophecy in Scripture ever came from the prophet's own understanding, or from human initiative. No, those prophets were moved by the Holy Spirit, and they spoke from God."

Just consider, for example, this powerful report:

He was despised and rejected—
a man of sorrows, acquainted with
deepest grief.
We turned our backs on him and looked
the other way.
He was despised, and we did not care.
Yet it was our weaknesses he carried;
it was our sorrows that weighed
him down.

And we thought his troubles were a
punishment from God,
a punishment for his own sins!
But he was pierced for our rebellion,
crushed for our sins.
He was beaten so we could be whole.
He was whipped so we could be healed.
All of us, like sheep, have strayed away.
We have left God's paths to follow
our own.
Yet the LORD laid on him
the sins of us all.

Would you like to venture a guess about who is being discussed? It's pretty clear, isn't it? It's a description, with detailed accuracy, of the suffering and crucifixion of the Messiah, Jesus Christ. What is remarkable is not so much the accuracy of the account, but the date when it was written: these words were penned by the Jewish prophet Isaiah (in Isaiah 53:3-6) *more than seven hundred years before the life and death of Christ*. And what's more, he predicted that Christ would be "pierced for our rebellion" centuries before crucifixion as a method of execution had even been invented. And in the last three verses of that chapter he even foreshadows the resurrection of Jesus. Read the passage for yourself! It's like a historical account—written in advance.

I'm confident that the more you spend time in the Bible—if you'll do so with a receptive heart and mind—the more you'll become convinced that it's not only a reliable record of what actually happened, but also a book that is truly inspired by God and beneficial to all of us who will read and heed it. As Jesus put it, "Blessed are all who hear the word of God and put it into practice" (Luke 11:28).

ARE WE ACCOUNTABLE TO GOD?

IT IS ENCOURAGING to come to the point at which you can acknowledge that the Bible is what it claims to be—God's Word, his revelation of truth, written for us. Doing so gives you the peace and assurance that comes with knowing God went out of his way to communicate with us, revealing himself as our loving heavenly Father.

But this is also challenging, because the Bible presents us with some very sobering realities. The first of those realities is that God is not only loving, but also *holy*. That word, *holy*, seems like sort of an old-fashioned one—we don't hear it much anymore. But the Bible presents it as a vitally important concept, because it tells us that God is absolutely pure and separate from anything that is tainted or stained by impurity, described in the Scriptures as sin.

This truth brings us face-to-face with a serious difficulty: God's standard of righteousness is something that none of us can live up to. Specifically, both the Old and New Testaments present a clear message from God that tells us, "You must be holy because I am holy."[1] The problem with that is obvious: we are *not* holy!

We are sinful people, plain and simple. Yes, the Bible says that originally we were created good; God does not create evil. But starting with the first human beings, right down to you and me, we have all rebelled against God in various ways. We've chosen our own path and ignored his will for our lives. We've become sinners.

Lest there be any doubt, just watch the daily news. The human race is marked by violence and immoral behavior, crimes large and small. Our wars destroy countless people—estimates say well over 100 million were killed in the twentieth century alone. Then there's the growing reality of terrorism, with its murder of innocent civilians, including women and children of all ages. Human trafficking and the growing worldwide sex trade. Governmental corruption. Corporate fraud. Immorality and abuse among clergy. Tax evasion, employee theft, students cheating on exams, job applicants lying on résumés. Abuse of our bodies, each other, and the planet. The stories and the statistics concerning our sinfulness are staggering.

The Bible predicted that society would become increasingly like this. Look at this prophetic description in 2 Timothy 3:2-5, written by the apostle Paul some 2,000 years ago:

For people will love only themselves and their money. They will be boastful and proud, scoffing at God, disobedient to their parents, and ungrateful. They will consider nothing sacred. They will be unloving and unforgiving; they will slander others and have no self-control. They will be cruel and hate what is good. They will betray their friends, be reckless, be puffed up with pride, and love pleasure rather than God. They will act religious, but they will reject the power that could make them godly.

It's easy to read a passage like that and say, "That's an awfully good depiction of the world as a whole, but it's not true of me. I don't do most of those things!" We tend to compare ourselves to other people, focusing on their worst sins versus our best attributes and concluding that in contrast to them we're really not so bad. But the Bible says that's a wrong comparison. God isn't asking whether we're better than the next man or woman; he tells us to "be holy because I am holy."

It's so easy to deceive ourselves. We look at our own life like a seemingly clean glass of water—one anyone would readily pick up and drink. But God has the power to examine that water through a microscope. He can see all the small but very real impurities suspended in the liquid. Specifically, he can see our impure thoughts, our mixed motives, our ugly envy, our insincere sentiments, our disingenuous gestures, and our service done for personal gain and recognition.

Worse, he sees our *pride*, which the Bible describes as being among the most destructive of all sins[2]—though it's the one that is often the most transparent to us. Ultimately it is our pride that convinces us that we're really not that bad; that we can work it all out; that we'll overcome our moral shortcomings; that we'll be okay in the end; that we really don't need God after all. And the people who struggle the least with the overt sins are often the ones who are most seduced and blinded by the hidden spiritual disease called pride.

C. S. Lewis explained the problem in *Mere Christianity*:

> *In God you come up against something which is in every respect immeasurably superior to yourself. Unless you know God as that—and, therefore, know yourself as nothing in comparison—you do not know God at all. As long as you are proud you cannot know God. A proud man is always looking down on things and people: and, of course, as long as you are looking down, you cannot see something that is above you.*[3]

In addition to the wrong things we've done, there's also the problem of the good things we've failed to do. For example, Jesus said in Matthew 22:37-38, "'You must love the LORD your God with all your heart, all your soul, and all your mind.' This is the first and greatest commandment." Confronted by such a lofty standard, can any of us claim to have lived up to that command throughout our entire lives? Have you put God first in everything? Nobody can authentically claim such perfection.

So in light of all the wrong things we've done, as well as all the right things we should have done but have not, I believe that every honest heart echoes the message of Romans 3:10 and 3:23: "No one is righteous—not even one. . . . For everyone has sinned; we all fall short of God's glorious standard."

. . .

A young man once asked Robert Laidlaw, "Do you think it is fair for God to set the standard of holiness so high that we cannot reach it and then judge us for falling short of it?"

He replied, "God has not set an arbitrary standard of holiness as an official sets an arbitrary standard of height for his bodyguards. In such a case, a man may have all the other qualifications, but if he is an inch too short he is disqualified.

"God has not really set a standard at all: He *is* the standard. He is absolute holiness, and to preserve his own character he must remain absolutely holy in all of his dealings with his creatures, maintaining that standard irrespective of the tremendous implications which it may hold for both him and us."

Some people have also suggested that all a person needs to do is sincerely reform, do better in the future, and thus live down past shortcomings. This is supposed to make one fit for heaven. But will it work?

Suppose the manager of a business goes to his accountant and discovers that his company owes $500,000 to the manufacturers and other suppliers. He says, "Write letters to all those people and tell them that we are no longer going to worry about the past, that we have turned over a new leaf, and that we promise to pay a hundred cents on the dollar in all future business, and from now on to live up to the highest standards of ethics."

The accountant would think his boss had lost his mind and would refuse to convey such a proposition to the creditors. Yet that's exactly what countless otherwise sane men and women are proposing to God—offering to try to meet their obligations toward him in the future, but refusing to worry about the past. But Ecclesiastes 3:15 (NIV) warns us that "God will call the past to account." Even if we assume we can somehow start living an absolutely perfect life—which is exactly what God's moral law demands (but which is impossible for us)—we would still be sinners.

God's righteous standards demand that no past accounts will be considered settled until they are paid to the last penny and every claim of justice is met. And if you think about it, our legal system works the same way: a murderer may cover his sin and live the life of a model citizen for ten or twenty years after his crime, but when he is discovered, the law will still condemn him. Though he hasn't hurt anyone for decades, it will still judge him as a murderer.

So, to merely hide past sins—including thoughts, words, or actions—with what seems to be an impeccably perfect life still leaves us sinners in the sight of the God to whom the past and the future are as visible as the present. According to his standard of holiness, we all have sinned, and we must all bring that sin out into the open to let him deal with it justly.

Justice is certainly what we deserve—and God must satisfy his own standards of justice—but thankfully he also offers us his mercy. Ultimately he gives us both justice and mercy by coming in the person of Jesus Christ to live a perfect life and then to clear the books for us by paying our debt himself. "Our friendship with God was restored by the death of his Son" (Romans 5:10). Amazingly, as we'll see in the discussion of the next question, Jesus laid down his life in place of ours that we could be forgiven and free.

• • •

For me, this all came together in my own understanding when I was nineteen years old. My conscience, my understanding of Scripture, and my sense of the Holy Spirit's "still, small voice" all compelled me to admit that I had fallen far short of God's standard of holiness and that, therefore, I was a sinner in his sight. No one who knew me at the time would have questioned that very obvious conclusion!

But with that realization came the further understanding of what the Bible says in Romans 6:23: "The wages of sin is death."

Laidlaw offers this illustration:

The law in Great Britain says that all drivers must keep to the left side of the street, while in New York the rule of the road demands that a driver keep to the right side. Now, suppose I go driving in London and keep to the right side. On being brought before the judge, I say, "This is ridiculous. In the United States we are allowed to drive on the right side."

"You are not being judged by the laws of America," he would reply. "It does not matter what the laws of other lands may be; you should have concerned yourself

only with the laws which judge you here, where you are."

In the same way, I was spiritually lost because God's standard was the one by which I was to be judged in eternity. I began to see that it didn't matter at all what I thought, what my friends told me, or even what society said. The judgment would be based on what *God* has said. Moreover, because in God's judgment we have all sinned, there was no use in looking to other people for help, because we were all in the same situation.

. . .

The Bible tells us Jesus came to bring us Good News—in fact, that's literally what the word *gospel* means. But before we can fully grasp how good that news really is, we need to understand the bad news of the predicament we all find ourselves in. As we've seen, Scripture tells us we all fall short of God's holy standard. And because he is not only holy but also *just*, he must ascribe to us the penalty we owe. That penalty is death—not just physical death, but spiritual death—which entails separation from God forever.

And to complete the sobering picture of the situation we're in, we are *morally bankrupt*, meaning we have nothing in our moral bank account—no spiritual reserves or merits—with which to pay the debt we owe.

Try as we might—and some of us try pretty hard—we can't earn our way back to God. In fact, when we realize the full perfection of God's holiness in contrast to our utter sinfulness, we realize that it would be foolish to even try.

These truths are hard to hear but extremely important to know. It's like being told you have a serious disease. That's bad news, but it can lead you to take action that can address your situation and prolong your life. Well, we all have a sin sickness, and left untreated, it will lead to certain spiritual death. Thankfully, there is a solution—a Savior—whom we'll talk about next.

WHO WAS JESUS AND WHAT WAS HIS PURPOSE?

THE SAME TRUSTWORTHY Bible that tells us about our sin also reveals our solution: Jesus Christ.

Maybe you've heard people say that Jesus never claimed to be the Son of God and that he'd roll over in his grave if he knew his followers today were worshiping him. Evidently, they never read what Jesus said—and they must have missed the news that he rose from the dead!

For example, in John 5:16-20, Jesus clearly paints himself as divine. This made his detractors so angry that they "tried all the harder to find a way to kill him." Why? Because Jesus "not only broke the Sabbath, he called God his Father, *thereby making himself equal with God*" (vs. 18, emphasis mine).

As the greatest teacher who ever lived, Jesus would have known if these people were misinterpreting his words and would have quickly corrected them if they were drawing the wrong conclusions. Instead, far from denying that he was "making himself equal with God," he went on to reinforce those claims.

You can read in John 8:56-59 how Jesus shook up his hearers again: "Your father Abraham rejoiced as he looked forward to my coming. He saw it and was glad." They were incredulous, saying, "You aren't even fifty years old. How can you say you have seen Abraham?"

They were stunned by what Jesus said next: "I tell you the truth, before Abraham was even born, I Am!" In one sentence, he claimed not only to exist before Abraham, but he applied the exclusive name of God—"I Am" (see Exodus 3:14)—to himself. His listeners got the point: either Jesus really was God in human flesh, or he was a blasphemer. They again opted for the second choice, picking up stones to kill him.

And in John 10:30-33, Jesus underscored this claim once more. He told his audience, "The Father and I are one." The original language makes it clear that he was claiming to be one in nature or essence with God, not merely unified in purpose. Without hesitating, his opponents picked up stones to kill him because "you, a mere man, claim to be God" (vs. 33).

Were they merely misunderstanding his claims? No, he was making it very clear that he was God's Son—deity living in humanity. Instead of correcting their misperceptions, he drove home again, in the verses that followed, how they could examine his works and his miracles in order to see that his claims were true (John 10:34-38). And another time he summed up in sobering terms why his identity was so important: "Unless you believe that I Am who I claim to be, you will die in your sins" (John 8:24).

Some skeptics point out that Jesus preferred to call himself the *Son of Man*, and they interpret that to mean that he was merely claiming to be human. For example, this was his most common self-reference in the Gospel of Mark, which was probably the earliest biography written about him.

After being asked by his accusers whether or not he was "the Messiah, the Son of the Blessed

One," he replied, "I Am. And you will see the Son of Man seated in the place of power at God's right hand and coming on the clouds of heaven" (Mark 14:61-62). Once again his opponents were horrified, accusing him of blasphemy and pronouncing him worthy of death.

Why? Because, first, it appears that Jesus was again using the divine name "I Am" to describe himself—something no mere human should ever do. Second, he said they would see him "seated in the place of power at God's right hand," which was a clear identification with the divine person described in Psalm 110:1. And third, he called himself "the Son of Man," which is a title drawn from Daniel 7:13-14, where the Son of Man was shown to possess divine characteristics. And just so there would be no doubt left in their minds, Jesus even said they would one day see him "coming on the clouds of heaven"—which means he would come back to judge humankind. This is another allusion to God in that same prophecy of Daniel (7:13).

Jesus' claims of equality with the Father were unmistakable, and they would have been blasphemy—had they not been *true*.

• • •

If Jesus Christ is the Son of God, then we may indeed be sure of the salvation he offers. But the difficulty still faces us: Is Jesus Christ really who he claimed to be? Many people have tried to limit the range of options concerning who he was to three: the Son of God, an honest but deluded man, or a deceiver. But there's a fourth option—one that more and more skeptics would embrace today—that he was a legend, or at least that his claims to deity were legendary. Let's look briefly at the three alternatives to his being who the Bible says he claimed to be, the Son of God.

First, was Jesus deluded? We find him matching wits with some of the cleverest people of his day, individuals who were sent to intentionally catch him in his words or in some factual mistake, and yet he so silenced them that they dared not ask him any more questions (Matthew 22:46). Even at the age of twelve he astounded the religious teachers with his spiritual insights. Luke 2:47 reports, "All who heard him were amazed at his understanding and his answers." And when we consider the wisdom of his teachings from an intellectual standpoint—for example, in his Sermon on the Mount (Matthew 5–7)—we see a simple brilliance that would suggest he was anything *but* deluded. On the contrary, both then and now, his influence has helped countless people to better face the realities of their own lives and to lift *them* out of delusion.

Or, second, was he trying to deceive people? If so, then he would have been acting in ways diametrically opposed to everything he stood for. Again, his enemies spent years following him around, critically weighing his every word and action in the hope of exposing some error or lie, but never with even a shred of success.

In fact, at the trial prior to his crucifixion it was ironically his accusers, not Jesus, who trumped up false charges. Matthew reports that they "were trying to find witnesses who would lie about Jesus, so they could put him to death" (Matthew 26:59). Mark adds, "But even then they didn't get their stories straight!" (14:59). So there was definitely some deception going on—but it was always against Jesus, never by him.

And look at the impact Jesus has had on people ever since then. Though his followers are not perfect as he was, his influence serves to make them more honest, trustworthy, and pure. He taught and modeled that we should always speak the truth, correct errors, and serve others selflessly. His earliest followers quickly became known for sharing their possessions, money, and meals with those in need; as a result they were "enjoying the goodwill of all the people" (Acts 2:44-47). This certainly does not sound like the influence that would flow from the life of a deceiver!

Third, might Jesus—or at least his claims to deity—have merely been legendary? As tempting as that option might be for some people today, it is fraught with fatal flaws. We've already explored the historical nature of the New Testament, including the Gospel accounts of Jesus' life and ministry. We've also discussed the wealth of early manuscript records we have of those writings—well beyond what we have for any other work of antiquity. In addition, there is strong secular confirmation for a number of the details in the biblical accounts.

Historian Gary Habermas, in his book *The Verdict of History*, reports thirty-nine ancient sources documenting the life of Jesus, from which he enumerates more than one hundred reported facts related to Jesus' life, teachings, crucifixion, and resurrection. Twenty-four of those sources, including seven secular sources and several creeds of the earliest church, specifically concern his divine nature. "These creeds reveal that the church did not simply teach Jesus' deity a generation later . . . because this doctrine is definitely present in the earliest church." The best explanation, he said, is that these creeds "properly represent Jesus' own teachings."[1]

No, the weight of history—both religious and secular—is on the side of Jesus being and doing exactly what the Bible reports about him: he was God in human flesh, who came to be the Savior of the world.

And as we've already seen, Jesus had many more "credentials" confirming his identity as the Son of God. These include his fulfillment of numerous messianic prophecies in the Old Testament, his morally impeccable life, his divine insights into human nature and even into the specific thoughts of the people he talked with, his miraculous works, and especially his resurrection from the dead—an event well documented by the eyewitnesses who knew the tomb was empty and who saw, talked, and even ate with the risen Jesus.[2]

. . .

So why did Jesus, the Son of God, come to live among us? What was his purpose? He tells us himself in the most famous verse in the Bible, John 3:16: "For God loved the world so much that he gave his one and only Son, so that everyone who believes in him will not perish but have eternal life." He saw that we were lost and that we had forfeited our lives to sin. But his life was not forfeited. It was sinless and spotless. He was willing to give this pure life in place of our sinful lives so that we could go free.

In fact, Jesus presented his personal mission statement in Luke 19:10. After explaining his offer of salvation to the inquisitive tax collector Zacchaeus, he declared, "The Son of Man came to seek and save those who are lost." And in

Mark 10:45 Jesus discussed his mission further: "Even the Son of Man came not to be served but to serve others and to give his life as a ransom for many."

In Philippians 2:6-11 the apostle Paul explains this in great depth and takes us to the very foundations of the Christian understanding of God's purposes:

Though he was God,
he did not think of equality with God
as something to cling to.
Instead, he gave up his divine privileges;
he took the humble position of a slave
and was born as a human being.
When he appeared in human form,
he humbled himself in obedience to God
and died a criminal's death on a cross.

Therefore, God elevated him to the place
of highest honor
and gave him the name above all
other names,
that at the name of Jesus every knee
should bow,

> in heaven and on earth and under
>   the earth,
> and every tongue confess that Jesus Christ
>   is Lord,
>   to the glory of God the Father.

Here's a brief explanation of what this passage tells us:

- *"He [Jesus] was God"* (vs. 6): Jesus made this claim himself in a number of different ways, his critics attacked and convicted him for blasphemy based on it, and the apostles and the early church embraced and consistently taught it.
- In spite of Jesus' divine nature, *"he did not think of equality with God as something to cling to."* This is a clear indicator of the biblical doctrine of the Trinity: there is one God who exists eternally in three persons. Jesus, the second person of the Trinity, didn't view the equal status he'd always had with the Father (the first person of the Trinity) as something to hold on to permanently.

- Rather, in light of Jesus' mission to redeem fallen humanity, he (vs. 7) *"gave up his divine privileges; he took the humble position of a slave and was born as a human being."* He did not lose or empty himself of deity—he always remained divine in nature—but he gave up his divine position and many of the perks that went with it, and he lowered himself to become one of us, with a genuine human nature. This is what we celebrate at Christmas: God incarnate.

- As if that wasn't enough, he even *"humbled himself in obedience to God [the Father] and died a criminal's death on a cross"* (vs. 8). Let that truth sink in a moment; it's almost beyond comprehension—the eternal Creator of the universe came down here as one of us, to die a dreadfully shameful and painful death *for us*.

- What could motivate the Almighty to come and suffer such humiliation and shame? Earlier, in verse 4, we're given a clue: Jesus was driven by *"an interest in others."* He did all of this for us out of *love*. He did it to pay the penalty we owed for the sins we've committed against him. No wonder people in churches have for centuries sung the classic English hymn that proclaims, "Amazing love! How can it be, that Thou, my God, shouldst die for me?"

· And what should our response be to this amazing love? Verses 10 and 11 tell us: *"At the name of Jesus every knee should bow . . . and every tongue confess that Jesus Christ is Lord, to the glory of God the Father."*

So Jesus is the Son of God—which means that he shares the divine nature of the heavenly Father from eternity past but that at his birth he became God incarnate, deity in human flesh. His coming was predicted by the prophet Isaiah more than seven hundred years ahead of time: "For a child is born to us, a son is given to us. . . . And he will be called . . . Mighty God" (Isaiah 9:6). And that child was born with the ultimate purpose of dying for us, as a "ransom" (Mark 10:45) or payment for our sins—in order to provide salvation for you and for me.

IS DIVINE FORGIVENESS AVAILABLE?

WHAT WE'VE SAID so far points strongly toward the conclusion that divine forgiveness *is* available, but how does it work? As we've discussed, Jesus died a criminal's death on the cross, but you might ask, "What does his death have to do with me now? How could such a tragic event 2,000 years ago possibly have any relevance for my life today?"

This question brings us to the core of the Christian faith. Let's think through the wisdom and the wonder of God's message of forgiveness for sinful people like us. In a word, it is salvation by *substitution*. Until we discover what it means for Christ to be our substitute, we won't really understand the gospel.[1] So we'll examine this question by considering three key points.

Our Moral Debt Must Be Paid

In the Bible's Old Testament, Ezekiel 18:20 tells us, "The person who sins is the one who will die." And in the New Testament, as we've already seen, Romans 6:23 warns us that "the wages of sin is death." Since we've all sinned, this tells us quite clearly that we all deserve the death penalty.

"But," some people will say, "why does any penalty have to be paid at all? Isn't God loving? Then why can't he just let us off the hook? Why can't God just 'forgive and forget'? Even I can do that! Can I do something that God can't do?"

I once met with two Muslims who were very serious about their beliefs. We were discussing the differences between Islam and Christianity when this central issue came up.

"Why do you believe that God has to make someone pay for our sins?" they asked. "And, in particular, why do you think it makes any sense that he would punish Jesus when *we're* the ones who have sinned?"

Then one of the men offered a poignant illustration of the problem. He looked over at the vase on my coffee table next to where they were sitting in my office. "If we were to break this beautiful vase," he said, "you probably wouldn't be very happy about it. But you seem like a gracious person, so you might just decide to forgive us and let us go our way. Correct? You could simply say, 'That's okay, even though you were a bit careless and you broke my favorite vase, I'm going to forgive you and forget about it; you're free to go your way.'"

I nodded, indicating that this was a realistic scenario.

"Well, if *you* can simply forgive and forget," he said, "then why can't God do the same thing? Is God incapable of doing something you are able to do so easily yourself?"

"And furthermore," the other man added, glancing at the picture of my family on the corner of my desk, "if we broke your vase and you forgave us, you surely would not then go home and punish your son in our place, would you? You wouldn't go and torture him, saying, 'Those guys broke my vase today, so now you, my son, are going to have to pay the penalty that they deserved!'"

It was obvious where this was headed, but I wanted to let them make their point.

"Yet that is exactly what you and most other Christians say about God," they continued. "Can't you see how wrong that teaching is? Where is there any justice in you forcing your son to pay a penalty for something that somebody else did? And, again, why does someone have to pay a penalty at all? Why can't a gracious God just forgive us and let it go at that? Well, we believe he can and often does—and this might help explain why we can't accept the teachings of Christianity."

The problem, as I sought to explain to them, was that their illustration was flawed. If they were to break the vase in my office, I could certainly say, "That's okay; I forgive you; you are free to go your way." But then *who would pay for the vase?* You see, I would have to fix or replace it myself, or go without it altogether, but I would still be bearing the cost, since I bought it in the first place. One way or another, the damage would have to be paid for, and I'd be left holding the bill.

In fact, anytime something is forgiven, the

person doing the forgiving must pay for the damages. If something tangible gets broken, stolen, or lost and you let the responsible person off the hook, then you have to cover the cost of it. This is also true if the damage is not tangible. If you are insulted or shamed by someone, for example, you can forgive the person who did that, but you must pay the price by enduring that insult or shame yourself.

Similarly, even though God wants to forgive and forget our sins—Micah 7:19 says that he wants to "throw them into the depths of the ocean"—he can do so only when the price has been paid, either by him or by us. That takes us back to the bad news I mentioned earlier: the price for our sins is death, and it would take us forever to try to pay off that debt—an eternity of spiritual separation from God. Thankfully, there is also good news.

God Paid the Price Himself

My Muslim friends were right about this at least: it would be cruel and unjust for me to forgive them for breaking my vase and then to go home and make my son pay for it—either through punishment or by extracting the money from him to replace it.

Yet that's how many people understand the message that Jesus died to pay for our sins. They say, "Where is the justice in having someone else be forced into the situation and then punished—or, as in the case of Jesus, tortured and put to death—in somebody else's place?" It's no wonder people who interpret the Christian message in this way have sometimes decried it as cosmic child abuse.

Some also compare it to a medieval practice involving something known as a whipping boy. When a young prince would break the rules, his tutors couldn't whip him because he was royalty. So instead they would bring in a young slave boy, and in the presence of the prince they would whip the slave boy in the prince's place. They would do this to show the prince that his offense was serious and that there was punishment to be paid. This was supposed to make the prince feel bad and help him change his attitude and behavior.

We hear about this today and recoil. How

could people have done such a thing? That is the view many have of Jesus dying on the cross, but here's the central problem with that view: they don't understand who Jesus really is.

This is vitally important: Jesus was *not* a reluctant third party or an uninvolved bystander forced by God onto the scene like a whipping boy in order to make him take our punishment. Rather, he is the God we've sinned against, and he willingly came to pay for our sins!

As we saw in Philippians 2, Jesus "was God," who out of love for us was willing to temporarily let go of his lofty position. "He gave up his divine privileges; he took the humble position of a slave and was born as a human being. When he appeared in human form, he humbled himself in obedience to God and died a criminal's death on a cross."

God, in keeping with his holy and just nature, said, in effect, "Either people will have to pay the penalty themselves—which will mean eternal death for them—or I've got to come and pay the death penalty in their place." So God, in keeping with his loving nature, willingly took on human flesh and, in the person of

Christ, died on the cross to pay the price that you and I owed for the sins we've committed. As Acts 20:28 puts it, we, the members of God's church, were "purchased with his own blood." Titus 2:14 adds, "He gave his life to free us from every kind of sin, to cleanse us, and to make us his very own people."

Robert Laidlaw illustrates this in a powerful way:

God acted like the judge in this story: Two young men studied law together, with one rising to a seat on the bench, while the other wasted his life through drugs and alcohol. This unfortunate fellow was brought before his old companion, charged with a crime. The lawyers wondered what kind of justice would be administered by the judge. Much to their surprise, he sentenced his onetime companion to the heaviest penalty the law allowed—but then he paid the fine himself, setting his old friend free.

Likewise God, against whom we have sinned, sat upon his throne and, in justice, passed his sentence upon us—and it was a

heavy one: death to all who have sinned.
Then, in mercy, he stepped from his throne
and in the person of Jesus Christ took our
place, bearing the full penalty himself.
That's why 2 Corinthians 5:19 tells us
"God was in Christ"—not through Christ
but in Christ—"reconciling the world to
himself, no longer counting people's sins
against them."

This explains why the concept of substitution is so central to Christianity. God substituted for us in Christ; he took our sin, he paid for it on the cross, he proved it was true when he came back to life three days later, and he lives today to give us his righteousness in exchange for our sin.

God Offers Us His Forgiveness as a Gift

God did all of this so that he could turn around and freely offer us his forgiveness, friendship, and leadership as a gift. We don't deserve it, we didn't pay for it, and we can't earn it. The only way we can receive it is to humbly bow before him, admit our waywardness, and say *yes* to his incredible offer.

And he says to you at this very moment, "I love you, I've willingly paid the penalty you owed, and I want to forgive you. Would you trust and follow me?"

When you do that, your sin-debt is paid in full, and you receive the promise of eternal life in heaven. You also gain the ongoing companionship of the gift giver himself, who will be there to lead, guide, and lovingly bring correction when you need it—for your own good and so you can better bring him honor as his beloved child.

That amazing message is summed up powerfully in these lines from a popular worship chorus: "He paid a debt He did not owe / I owed a debt I could not pay / . . . Christ Jesus paid a debt that I could never pay."

We'll discuss in more detail how we can access this incredible gift—this "Amazing Grace"—but first let's address several questions that sometimes arise when people hear this message of the gospel, the Good News.

• • •

Couldn't God have saved us another way? We had broken his law and the penalty was death. How could Jesus have delivered us without paying our full penalty? If he paid anything less than the complete price, then there would still be judgment for us to face ourselves. But because he did die and pay the death penalty that each of us owed, the law we had broken could no longer judge us.

That's why the Bible says, "So now there is no condemnation for those who belong to Christ Jesus. . . . God declared an end to sin's control over us by giving his Son as a sacrifice for our sins. He did this so that the just requirement of the law would be fully satisfied for us" (Romans 8:1, 3-4).

Robert Laidlaw tells the story of a court case that was extended into a second day:

As is the usual practice, the jurors were kept in custody overnight so no outside influence could affect their decision. But upon entering the court the next morning, the judge said to them: "Men and women, the case is dismissed: the prisoner has been called to a higher court." The accused had died in the jail cell during the night so there was no use going on with the case, since the law cannot judge a dead person.

Consider this: If someone murders one person he may be given the death penalty, but if he murders six people he can still only be put to death, because that is the utmost penalty of the law. No matter what someone's sins may be, the law knows no greater penalty than to take that person's life.

Therefore, it doesn't matter that there are sins in my life I have long since forgotten. I don't have to be afraid of them, because I'm confident that Jesus, my Substitute, already suffered the utmost penalty of the law on my account, freeing me absolutely from all its claims against me—both great and small.

• • •

If Christ died for all, then can we assume that everyone will be saved? God does not say that. He says there is salvation for all, not that all people will actually receive that salvation.

Here is another helpful illustration from Laidlaw:

> *It is a bitterly cold winter and unemployment is rife in one of our great cities, with many in dire need. The government is providing free meals. You meet a down-and-out person on the street who tells you he is starving. Naturally, you ask if he believes the notices that are posted all over the city explaining that there is enough food for everyone—and being provided for free.*
>
> *"Yes," he replies. "I suppose I believe it, but I am still hungry."*
>
> *You explain that he is sure to remain hungry, in spite of the food that has been provided, unless he goes and eats and drinks personally of what is being offered to everyone in need.*
>
> *Just the same, although the death of Jesus provides* potential *salvation for everyone,*[2] *only those who believe that he*

died in their place and personally receive him will be saved. We must take Jesus as our Savior, or his death will do nothing for us—just as a person could die of thirst beside a spring of water if he refused to make its life-giving stream his own by drinking of it himself.

• • •

How could Jesus' one life be considered the substitute for the lives of so many, so that God can offer salvation to everyone who places their faith in him? Laidlaw again:

That's a fair question—a problem that a bit of arithmetic can help answer. Christ was, as we discussed earlier, "God incarnate"—Divinity in humanity—so that the life he gave was infinite, which can meet the needs of any number of finite lives.

Get a sheet of paper and write down all the big figures you can think of—trillions or more—and add them up. Now that you have a really big number, multiply it by another 10,000—or a billion or a trillion, if you like. Fill up sheets of paper with repeated multiplication, and after that you still have a finite number, a number that is bound by a beginning and an end, however far it may extend. No, by adding finite things together you'll never be able to make something that is infinite. The infinite life of Christ given for us is more than sufficient to save all who receive him as the One who died for them.

Or, as the Bible puts it, "Christ died for sins once for all, the righteous for the unrighteous, to bring you to God" (1 Peter 3:18, NIV).

• • •

How could Christ suffer for my sins when they were not committed until 2,000 years after he died? At first this seems like a serious problem, but there is a solution. God is all-knowing, and he is eternal. In Exodus 3:14, God calls himself "I Am" (present tense), and as we saw, Jesus said in John 8:58, "Before Abraham was even born, I Am" (again, present tense). In other words, to one who knows all things and is eternal, time is not an issue. Events that will take place 2,000 years from now are as clear to God as events that happened 2,000 years ago, and both are as clear to him as events happening now.

More specifically, Romans 3:25-26 explains that: "God presented Jesus as the sacrifice for sin. People are made right with God when they believe that Jesus sacrificed his life, shedding his blood. This sacrifice shows that *God was being fair when he held back and did not punish those who sinned in times past*, for he was looking ahead and including them in what he would do in this present time."[3] So Jesus' death on the cross was, in effect, a timeless event that covered the sins of all who would trust in God's gracious provision for them—both BC and AD.[4]

• • •

If God knows what will happen ahead of time, then isn't it already predetermined—leaving us with no choice about it? Not at all. The Bible makes it clear that God does know the beginning from the end, including what we will choose to do. But it is also clear that we make real decisions, including what we'll do with God's generous offer of salvation provided through the death of Christ. For example, look at the open invitation God gives to all people: "The Spirit and the bride say, 'Come.' Let anyone who hears this say, 'Come.' Let anyone who is thirsty come. Let anyone who desires drink freely from the water of life" (Revelation 22:17).

So when you add these truths together, you begin to understand that God foreknows what we will one day freely do, and if you decide to do otherwise, he already knew that you would choose *that* course of action. Further, he holds us responsible for the actual choices we make and rewards us accordingly. So if you'll choose to follow Christ, God won't be surprised, but he will be pleased and will welcome you home with open arms!

• • •

Why didn't God just make us incapable of disobeying his will and therefore unable to sin? That's like asking why God does not draw a crooked straight line or a square circle, or make an object blue all over and red all over at the same time. Humans are, by our very nature, creatures with the power of intelligent choice, so the question really is this: *Why didn't God make a creature with the power of intelligent choice and yet without the power of intelligent choice at the same time?*

Let's say I was capable of mind control and could put my children in a trance, robbing them of the power of intelligent choice. Then I could tell them, "Sit on that couch until I return"; "Get up and eat now"; "Stop eating so many sweets"; or even "Give me a goodnight hug"—and they would do exactly what they were told. They would stay where I told them, they would eat and stop eating as instructed, and unfeeling arms would go around my neck, mechanically squeezing me close to them. I would have prompt and perfect obedience to my every command, but would it mean anything? Of course not.

I want *real* children—kids with free wills, who are capable of disobeying me, but who willingly choose to honor my instructions, which flow out of my love for them and are given for their own good.

Likewise, God does not want puppets that will jump in a given direction according to the string that is pulled, nor does he want robots who have the physical form of humans but who mechanically obey his every wish. Rather, God wants *real* children—people who can reject his love, but who can also choose to truly love him in return. Real love always entails choice. One of the reasons I know my wife, Heidi, genuinely loves me is because she doesn't have to—but thankfully she freely chooses to do so!

Human beings are truly magnificent creatures, far above the animal creations around us. There is a great gulf between the highest animals and ordinary humans, because God has given us the awesome power of being able to say no to him as well as a genuine yes. And, in your own interest, let me encourage you to say yes to God—even as you are reading this book.

• • •

What does God care about this little world of ours compared with the vastness of the mighty universe? The Hubble Space Telescope has allowed us to see into the depths of space as we never have before, revealing the existence, according to astrophysicist Hugh Ross, of some "200 billion galaxies in the observable universe . . . [which] contain, on average, about 200 billion stars each. So the total number of stars in these galaxies adds up to about 40 billion trillion—and that's without the estimated 10 billion trillion stars contained in the unobserved dwarf galaxies."[5] And more recent reports suggest that the universe might actually contain three times as many stars as was believed when the above description was written. That would give us a grand total of 300,000,000,000,000,000,000,000 stars (give or take), or a number described as 300 sextillion![6]

Somewhere in the midst of all of that is our tiny planet.

Of what value can Earth be to God, and of how much less importance can people be? That was the question Laidlaw described an astronomer having asked himself as his childhood faith evaporated. The vastness of the universe had robbed him of his faith in his parents' God. *How long could God trouble himself with people, who by comparison are smaller than a grain of sand?* he wondered.

But his thirst for knowledge would not let him rest. The heavens were available for study by telescope only at night, so how should he spend the free hours of the day? Why not with a microscope? Suddenly, new worlds were opened to him at his fingertips—worlds as wonderful as those above—and slowly his faith returned. Yes, the God who could attend to such minute details as to make a drop of ditch water throb with infinitesimal life was sure to be interested in humans, the highest form of his creation. So the astronomer found balance instead of bias, and that balance helped bring him back to God.

James Tour, nanoscientist at Rice University, said, "I stand in awe of God because of what he has done through his creation. . . . Only a rookie who knows nothing about science would say science takes away from faith. If you really study science, it will bring you closer to God."[7] As the psalmist King David puts it, "When I look at the night sky and see the work of your fingers— the moon and the stars you set in place—what are mere mortals that you should think about them, human beings that you should care for them? Yet you made them only a little lower than God and crowned them with glory and honor" (Psalm 8:3-5).

• • •

Can faith really make sense in this age of reason? Yes. In fact, wise faith and reason go hand in hand—and depend on each other. What is faith? I describe it as "belief and action based on something we consider trustworthy," and in that sense everyone has faith—in something![18] It's true that Christians have faith in Christ, and Buddhists put their trust in the teachings of the Buddha, but atheists and agnostics have faith too! They believe and act based on what they consider to be reliable reasons to think there is no God. They can't *prove* he doesn't exist, but they live their lives trusting that to be the case and believing that there will be no judgment day at which they'll be held accountable for what they did in this life.

But ultimately any faith is only as good as what it trusts in. And the evidence, as I've summarized it, points powerfully to the existence of the God of the Bible and to his role in creating the universe. It also points to the reality of his entering our world in the person of Jesus in order to lovingly "seek and save those who are lost" (Luke 19:10).

So the wise course is to study that information with an open mind and then take appropriate action on what you learn—which I'm convinced will entail putting your faith in the God who loves you and who came to redeem you.

. . .

But why should God judge my sins as worthy of death? I'm not sure we can fully answer that question, but I would suggest that because of God's infinite holiness, no sin can exist indefinitely in his presence. And because of his infinite justice, he must ultimately punish those who persist in rejecting him and his moral standards.

The Bible tells us that "God is light, and there is no darkness in him at all" (1 John 1:5). The more we can grasp this, the more we understand God's need to punish sin.

God's attributes of holiness and justice were exhibited throughout Old Testament history as he prescribed animal sacrifices by God's people as a way to temporarily cover their sins. This practice powerfully illustrated the fact that sin is serious and deserving of God's punishment—and that the penalty for sin is death. It also presented a picture of the principle of substitution, in that an animal could bear the punishment in place of the penitent sinner.[9]

But what was foreshadowed by the repeated sacrifices of animals in the Old Testament was fulfilled in the New Testament by the appearance of Jesus—whom John the Baptist introduced to the world as "the Lamb of God who takes away the sin of the world" (John 1:29). We are further told in Hebrews that Jesus paid for our sins "once for all when he offered himself as the sacrifice for the people's sins" (Hebrews 7:27).

So that at least in part answers the question above—and it reinforces the good news that you have a Savior who has already died in your place to pay for those sins.

• • •

*It may be just, but is it merciful of God to refuse
to take us all to heaven, even if we reject Christ
and his payment on the cross for our sins?* Yes,
I believe it is both just and merciful. Would it
be kindness and mercy on God's part to bring
somebody who was still in their sins into the
holy light of heaven if that person had rejected
his offer of forgiveness and salvation for their
entire life?

Think about this: if you and I would not
want to allow our friends to see inside our minds
to read all the thoughts and see all the images
that have ever been there (and our friends' standards are probably no higher than our own),
then what would it be like to stand before God,
whose absolute holiness would reveal our sin in
all of its unedited ugliness?

Revelation 6:16 describes the desperate feel-
ings of people who have refused to receive Jesus
as their Savior but who, still in their sins, are
about to face God: "And they cried to the moun-
tains and the rocks, 'Fall on us and hide us from
the face of the one who sits on the throne.'" Yet

it is the presence of this same Christ that will turn eternity into heaven for those who have received him as their forgiver and leader.

So do you see the absurdity of talking about God taking us all to heaven? Heaven is a condition as well as a place. The presence of Jesus Christ will constitute heaven to those who have been cleansed from their sins, at the same time as it would make a hell of remorse in the hearts of those who, still stained by sin, were forced to stand in the infinite light of his holiness. Let's be honest—could you really be happy in the presence of the One whose love you had rejected and whose great sacrifice on the cross you had counted unworthy of your acceptance?

• • •

We've now seen numerous reasons why we can be confident that:

There is a God;

The Bible is a trustworthy revelation from him;

We are accountable to God for the sins we've committed;

Jesus is the unique Son of God who came
    to earth to "give his life as a ransom" in
    order to pay our penalty and secure our
    salvation; and

God's divine forgiveness has been
    graciously made available to you
    and to me.

In the final section I want to address the critically important question of how we can access that forgiveness—and all God has for us.

WHAT DO
I NEED TO DO?

"You Might Be Rich" and not even know it. So screams the title of a *Dateline NBC* series of television programs, as well as countless websites and online advertisements. According to the reports, there are millions of dollars in unclaimed funds throughout the United States, with a total of some $33 billion on hold, "being safeguarded by state treasurers and other agencies for 117 million accounts,"[1] and who knows how much in all the other nations of the world? Can you imagine? Untold wealth, just waiting for its rightful owners to step up and claim it!

As exciting as that might seem, it pales in comparison to the value of the unclaimed spiritual treasures that await those of us who receive

God's amazing gift of grace. Here's one of the places where the Bible describes it:

> *But God is so* rich in mercy, *and he loved us so much, that even though we were dead because of our sins, he gave us life when he raised Christ from the dead. . . . So God can point to us in all future ages as examples of* the incredible wealth of his grace and kindness toward us, *as shown in all he has done for us who are united with Christ Jesus. (Ephesians 2:4-5, 7, emphases mine)*

Just as in the case of the unclaimed money, however, people won't benefit from this wealth unless they know about the resources available to them and take the steps necessary to access those resources. That's why this last section of *The Reason Why* is so important. We've already seen that Christ came to purchase our salvation on the cross, as our substitute. The price has been paid; God's forgiveness and eternal life have been made available. But what must we do to personally access them?

Our instinctive answer is that we're going to have to work for it. It is ingrained in our very nature as human beings:

If it's worth anything, it'll cost something.

If you want to have it, you've gotta earn it.

We work hard to pay off our debts and to get ahead. Then we find out we owe a spiritual debt—as Romans 3:23 and 6:23 put it, "Everyone has sinned; we all fall short of God's glorious standard. . . . The wages of sin is death." So how do we react? We start trying to pay back those wages and earn our way back into God's good graces. "If I can just live a little cleaner, work a little harder, give a little extra, pray a little longer—then God will be impressed, and he'll overlook all the bad things I've done."

And in the process we miss the point: *God is offering us the greatest gift ever given!*

A friend of mine illustrates this well. We began with an illustration about engagement rings, and we'll close with another. He tells us to imagine a man who loved a woman deeply and wanted to marry her. So he took a family heirloom that had been handed down to him—a priceless diamond ring—and on the evening of the proposal offered it to her as a symbol of his love and commitment.

"Oh, it's beautiful!" she exclaimed. "But I could never take something of such great value as a gift. Let me help pay for it." And with that, she opened her purse and handed her dismayed fiancé a twenty-dollar bill.

This woman made two big mistakes: First, she insulted her fiancé by trying to pay for something offered to her freely as a gift. And second, she offended him by thinking that a measly twenty dollars would even begin to approach the value of what he was trying to give to her.

We can learn from her mistakes. God is offering us a gift of grace. Grace, by definition, is free and unmerited. We can't do anything to earn or pay for it. And if we could, the price would be far higher than anything we've ever tried to do for God—or can even imagine doing.

This natural, works-oriented approach is what has been called the "DO Plan."[2] It tells us to do a lot of good things and hopefully, if we do enough, we'll gain divine forgiveness and favor. Almost every religion is built on some variation of this plan, including some confused versions of Christianity.

As with the ring scenario, there are two serious problems with this plan: First, you'll never feel you've done enough. It's like running in a race that has no finish line. You can run faster and farther, but you'll never know if or when you've run far enough. That's the tyranny—and the futility—of performance-based religion. Second, God tells us repeatedly in the Bible that we never *can* do enough. As we saw in Romans 3:23, regardless of the intensity of our efforts we still fall short of God's perfect standard.

So the DO Plan fails every time. Thankfully, there's an alternative that has been ordained by God himself: the "DONE Plan." It's named that because Jesus has *done* for us what we could never do for ourselves: he lived a sinless human life and then died to pay the penalty we owe for our sinfulness. Ephesians 2:8-9 explains that this payment is a gift that is given freely to those who believe:

God saved you by his grace when you
believed. And you can't take credit for this;
it is a gift from God. Salvation is not a
reward for the good things we have done,
so none of us can boast about it.

It's an expensive gift, paid for in full by God himself, which we don't deserve and could never earn—so we can't take credit for it or brag about it.

God, through Christ, has DONE everything necessary to provide and offer it. But let's get really practical. If we can't earn it, then how can we make this gift our own?

Fortunately, this question is answered in the words of John 1:12: "But to all who believed him and accepted him, he gave the right to become children of God." This verse presents three components for a sound faith:

Believe + Accept = Become

The first word is *believe*. The verse begins: "But to all who believed him . . ." The message is that you can carefully check out Jesus' credentials in order to know that he is who he claimed to be and therefore merits your trust. This is the intellectual side of faith—coming to the point of confidence that he really is the unique Son of God and Savior of the world. This was much of the focus of the beginning of this book.

Unfortunately, many people gain that confidence but then stop cold. They nod their heads in agreement with the right ideas, but they never take the next step and express real faith. Many of them even go to church and become religious non-Christians. This is much like going to an airport full of knowledge about the science of aviation but never actually flying. You'd have the right beliefs, but they wouldn't get you anywhere.

The second word is *accept*. The verse says: "But to all who believed him *and accepted him* . . ."[3] Returning to the airport example, genuine faith doesn't just nod its head to the theory of flight; it puts that belief into action by climbing on board an airplane and actually going somewhere. Similarly, Scripture tells us we need to not only believe the truth about Jesus, we also must accept him and what he offers us. This is how we receive the gift of salvation—by humbly admitting our need for it and asking him for his forgiveness and leadership.

To do so is not to earn anything; receiving a gift is not the same as working for it. Rather, it's like Christmas: God is handing you his gift of salvation. All that's left for you to do is to reach out and receive it. If you refuse to do so, then the gift, though offered freely, will not be yours. But if you'll humbly *accept* that gift, then it will become your own.

The third word in the faith "formula" is *become*. The Bible makes it clear that when we sincerely believe in the claims of Jesus and then accept him as our forgiver and leader, at that moment we are cleansed of all our sins and we become his adopted son or daughter.

That simple step is what it takes to become a true Christian—a forgiven child of God. What comes after that? A life of adventure as you follow and serve him, doing, as it says in Ephesians 2:10, "the good things he planned for us," not as a way to try to pay for or earn what you've already been given, but out of love and gratitude to the One who freely gave it to you.

But is the acceptance of Christ as my forgiver and leader all that is necessary to save me for eternity?

"Yes," explains Laidlaw:

Though I'll admit the simplicity of it seems to make it hard to grasp. But if I owe $100,000 and have nothing with which to pay, and a friend pays the debt for me and gives me the receipt, I don't need to worry about it any longer. I can look my creditor straight in the face, for I hold his signed receipt. When Jesus Christ gave his life in place of mine, he said, "It is finished," meaning that the work of atonement was completed, and God gave me his receipt. The assurance that God was satisfied with Christ's finished work is that he raised Christ from the dead on the third day.

"But I can't see it," said a cabinetmaker, as his friend tried to explain this to him. At last, an idea came to the friend. Lifting a piece of sandpaper menacingly, he acted as if he was going to sand the top of a beautifully polished table that stood nearby.

"Stop!" cried the cabinetmaker. "Can't you see that table is finished? You'll ruin it if you use that sandpaper on it!"

"That," replied his friend, "is exactly what I have been trying to explain to you about Christ's work of redemption. It was finished when he gave his life for you, and if you try to add to that finished work you will only spoil it. Just accept it as it stands—his life for yours—and you will go free."

Like a flash the cabinetmaker saw it and received Jesus Christ into his life as his Savior.

• • •

"But," says someone, "I know a successful and sophisticated leader who is not a Christian and is very open about that fact, and I know a rather simple and unsophisticated laborer who is a Christian and who shows his belief in many ways. Do you mean to tell me God prefers the unsophisticated person just because he had accepted Christ as his Savior?"

Laidlaw comments:

*This question arises from a confusion of
ideas. A Christian is not different in degree
from a non-Christian; he is different
in kind, just as the difference between
a diamond and a cabbage is not one of
degree, but of kind. The one is polished and
the other plain; but the polished one is dead
while the plain one is alive! Therefore the
polished one does not have what the other
one has—life—in any degree whatsoever.
Such is the difference that God sees between
a Christian and non-Christian.*

The Bible explains: "And this is what God has testified: He has given us eternal life, and this life is in his Son. Whoever has the Son has life; whoever does not have God's Son does not have life" (1 John 5:11-12).

So the vital and all-important question for each of us is not "am I sophisticated or unsophisticated," but rather, "am I alive or dead towards God?" In other words, "Have I received God's risen Son who brings me the life God offers? Or have I rejected him and remained one who does not have real life?"

• • •

If I believe Jesus Christ gave his life in place of mine, and that by receiving him I may have salvation, will perceiving these facts in a cold, mechanical way give me everlasting life?

Laidlaw answers with passion:

Certainly not! Two people can be forced or coerced into "marriage," and even go through the motions of a marriage ceremony, but are their hearts really knit together? Of course not. In order for a man and a woman to truly be one they must love in such a way as to receive each other into the innermost recesses of their hearts, in such a deep and true way that they cannot fully put into words all that they feel.

We all have those inner recesses, which are sacred to us, where emotions stir that no one else could possibly understand. Jesus Christ, God's Son, claims the right to enter there. The love he had shown for us entitles him to that place. Will we withhold it?

When I think that Christ's love for me was so great that he left his Father's glory and came to earth to die in my place and give me eternal life, my heart softens towards him.

If I were lying injured and helpless in a burning building and a friend rushed in to save me, wrapping blankets around me in a way that protected me from harm, but in the process he was critically burned and scarred himself, don't you think my heart would go out to him? God knows it would!

And now I am face-to-face with my Savior. *I can see him suffering in the Garden of Gethsemane in anticipation of his death on the cross for me. I see him in Pilate's judgment hall; the soldiers have been striking him in the face, saying, "Prophesy to us! Who hit you that time?" I see them crowning him with a crown of thorns. They take him bleeding and bruised from judgment to Calvary, where they drive spikes through his hands and his feet. As he is then lifted up to die between two thieves, the people gather around to mock and ridicule him, though he is pouring out his life to redeem them. Then I begin to understand what self-sacrificing love really means as I hear him cry, over and over, right up until his final breath, "Father, forgive them, for they don't know what they are doing."*

But even if we could enter into the physical sufferings of Christ until tears streamed down our cheeks, and that was all, we still would have failed miserably to comprehend the true significance of the cross. We read in 2 Corinthians 5:21 that "God made Christ, who never sinned, to be the offering for our sin, so that we could be made right with God through Christ." Come with me, I beg you, with bowed head and humbled heart, and let us enter into the soul-sufferings of Christ the Son, and of God the Father, as that Holy One, who hated sin as we would hate disease or death, is made to become "the offering for our sin."

If the higher the development of the physical organism the greater the capacity for pain, then the higher the development of the moral character the greater the capacity for soul-suffering. So just imagine *what sin must be like in all its awfulness to an absolutely holy God! Now we understand why, in the Garden of Gethsemane, Christ turns in utter disgust from sin and cries out in agony of soul, "My Father! If it is possible, let this cup of suffering be taken away from me. Yet I want your will to be done, not mine" (Matthew 26:39). In spite of that agonized plea from Gethsemane it's still true that "God loved the world so much that he gave his one and only Son"—"the offering for our sin"—"so that everyone who believes in him will not perish but have eternal life" (John 3:16; 2 Corinthians 5:21).*

Now do you understand *why I dare not reject One who has endured so much*

for me? My mind is convinced that it
is true; my emotions have been deeply
stirred; and now they both appeal to my
will for a decision. To be true to my God
and myself and my eternal future I have
only one course open, and I must take it.
Today I'll make Jesus Christ my forgiver
and leader; my Savior and Lord.

• • •

That was the decision that I needed to make
when I was nineteen years old. As I described
earlier, I grew up being taught the truth about
God, Jesus, and Christ's death for us on the
cross. I understood at least in a general way that
there was evidence backing up these beliefs, and
so, going back to the faith formula of John 1:12
(*Believe* + *Accept* = *Become*), I had the *believe* part
pretty much worked out.[4]

That may or may not be the situation for
you. Perhaps you still have some serious questions or doubts about the veracity of the case for
Christianity. If so, I'd recommend finishing the
last few pages of this book and then immediately

reading it again, as I'm confident that the information in the earlier portions will be clearer and stronger in your understanding the second time through. I'd also recommend reading books that address this information in a bit more depth—books such as my *Choosing Your Faith . . . In a World of Spiritual Options*, Josh and Sean McDowell's *More Than a Carpenter*, and Lee Strobel's *The Case for Christ*. These books will present you with deeper but highly readable overviews of the powerful evidence that supports Christianity.

I'm confident of this: the deeper you look—assuming you'll read with a receptive mind and an open heart—the more you'll become persuaded concerning the basic claims of the Christian faith. I say this because after more than three decades of studying both the attacks against that faith and the evidence for it, I'm surer than ever that it is based on real facts. In short, I'm convinced that Christianity is *true*.

For me the harder part of the faith formula was the second element: the need to *accept*. That's because I intuitively understood that I would be accepting not just the forgiveness that was available to me, but also the Forgiver. I knew that he would not be satisfied to simply deal with my past sins and weak spiritual performance—he would also want to begin guiding my life into the future. In other words, Christ wanted to be my forgiver *and* my leader.

I didn't like this at first because I knew my life would need to change. But then gradually God began to open my eyes to the fact that his ways are better! That the old ways I would be giving up were destructive ways—not just unpleasing to him, but also unhealthy for me. I began to understand what should not be shocking once one realizes he or she is dealing with the Creator of the universe: God knows what's best for me, and because he loved me before I even knew him (Romans 5:8-11), he has my best interests in mind.

And so, with this growing awareness, I finally reached the point where I could wholeheartedly accept his salvation and guidance—and I must tell you now, years later, that those realizations were right; God's ways *are* best for us. He does have our best interests in mind. No, following him is not always easy; sometimes it can be much harder. But it's ultimately better. And the benefits I've discovered in this life, I'm sure, are nothing compared to those in the next.

So how about you? Do you *believe*? Then why not *accept*, as well? His ways are better for you, too—he loves you, and he wants to forgive you and to guide you into becoming all that he made you to be. Believing and accepting is the only way to *become* a true son or daughter of God. You'll be glad you did—both in this life and in the best one, to come.

How can you do this? Just come to God and say—silently or out loud—a prayer like this:

> *God, I don't understand the mystery of it all. I can't comprehend why you would care enough for me to send Jesus Christ to pay the penalty of my sins. But with all my lack of understanding, I am willing to yield to you completely. I trust in Jesus' death for me, and I believe he rose to give us new life. I accept the promise you made in John 3:16, which tells us, "Everyone who believes in him will not perish but have eternal life."*

*I do believe, Lord, and I accept all that
you have for me: your forgiveness, your
leadership, and your help through life's ups
and downs. I want to become your child.
I am yours—body, mind, and soul—and
I know that you are mine. Thank you for
forgiving my sins and, even now, starting
to guide me into this new life. In Jesus'
name, Amen.*

Then record your decision—for yourself and for
anyone else you might want to tell—by signing
the declaration that follows.

MY DECISION

Before God, who knows me inside and out, I *believe* that Jesus Christ is the Son of God, who came into the world to seek and to save people who were spiritually lost—including me. Further, I *accept* Jesus into my life as my forgiver and leader, Savior and Lord. I yield my life to him and him alone. I know, on the basis of his words in John 1:12, that I have now *become* his child. And according to Jesus' message in John 5:24, I know I have already received everlasting life:

> *I tell you the truth, those who listen to my message and believe in God who sent me have eternal life. They will never be*

condemned for their sins, but they have already passed from death into life.

Signed: _____

Date: _____

NEXT STEPS

IF YOU JUST MADE that decision and prayed that prayer, let me be the first to say *congratulations*! You've made the best choice you could ever make and received the greatest gift ever given. Now make sure you tell a mature Christian friend or two—even today, if possible—so they can celebrate with you and encourage you in your new relationship with Christ. (Please also let me know by shooting a brief e-mail to ReasonWhyStories@gmail.com.)

It's important to get involved right away in a community of believers—a church—that will help you grow in your faith. Make sure it's one that agrees with the biblical teachings you've been reading in this book, including the inspiration and authority of the Bible, the full deity as well as humanity of Jesus (and the vitally important doctrine of the Trinity, which we discussed earlier: one God who exists eternally in three persons, Father, Son, and Holy Spirit), and in salvation by faith in Christ alone.

Also, try to read at least a chapter in the New Testament each day from a clear and reliable translation of the Bible (like the *New Living Translation*, the NLT, which I've been quoting throughout this book), asking God to speak to you, guide you, teach you, and use you for his purposes.

Get in the habit of talking to God regularly, admitting any sins you're struggling with (see 1 John 1:9), asking him for help and guidance, thanking him for his gifts and blessings, and worshiping him, which is always appropriate.

You're on a brand-new adventure!

POSTSCRIPT:
THE SOLDIER'S CHOICE

ROBERT LAIDLAW often worked to spiritually encourage people in the military during WWI and WWII. One day he was seeking to help a young soldier understand and receive Jesus Christ, but the man was trying to put off the issue with the promise, "I'll think it over."

Now, sometimes it's appropriate to encourage people to do just that—especially those who lack information or who have doubts about the basic claims of Christianity. But Laidlaw sensed that this situation was different, that this young man really did understand the message. Going back to the faith formula, it seemed he clearly did *believe*, but was resisting the natural next step, which is to *accept*. So Laidlaw decided to take it a bit further.

"Harry," he said, "let me offer an illustration: You are out with your comrades one night scouting an enemy post. On the way back your unit gets hit hard, and you're badly wounded. Another soldier sees the situation and stops long enough to pick you up and carry you to your own lines, but for his efforts he gets two bullets in the back. You are both taken to the hospital and through the best of medical care are brought back from the very edge of death.

"Two months later your doctor brings in a soldier who limps badly and moves with obvious pain. They stop by your bedside, and the doctor says, 'Harry, I want to introduce you to Bill Smith, the man who nearly lost his life in order to save yours.' But you fold your arms, look away, and say, 'I'm not sure I want to meet him. I'll think it over.'

"Now, you wouldn't say that, would you? No, once you knew that this was the man who had risked everything to save your life, you would grab his arm and do everything you could to express to him the gratitude you now felt.

"Harry, today I want to introduce you to Jesus Christ, the Man who not only risked his life, but who actually sacrificed it in order to save you. And you propose to turn your back on him and say you'll think it over?"

"No," he said, "I'll accept him." Together they prayed while Harry told the Lord that he, in that very moment, wanted to receive Jesus as his very own Savior.

Are you "thinking it over," or have you faced the issue squarely and decided to do what you now know to be right?

Notes

Introduction

1. Today this chain of department stores is better known by the shorter name, "Farmers." See www.farmers.co.nz.

2. There are two books that offer a wealth of information about Laidlaw and *The Reason Why*. The first is Ian Hunter's *Robert Laidlaw: Man for Our Time* (Auckland, New Zealand: Castle Publishing, Ltd., 1999); the second is Robert A. Laidlaw's autobiographical *The Story of "The Reason Why"* (Grand Rapids, MI: Zondervan, 1969). The latter one also gives fascinating details about Laidlaw's work among the Allied troops, mostly in the UK, during WWII.

Matters of Faith Really Matter

1. This description of our bodies "turning to dust" is from an earthly perspective. We also know from Scripture that our bodies will one day be raised again, before the judgment. See, for example, 1 Corinthians 15:35-58, especially verse 42: "It is the same way with the resurrection of the dead. Our earthly bodies are planted in the ground when we die, but they will be raised to live forever."

2. See Mark 9:23-25.

Is There a God?

1. Norman L. Geisler and Frank Turek, *I Don't Have Enough Faith to Be an Atheist* (Wheaton, IL: Crossway Books, 2004).

2. Rudolf Bultmann, et al, *Kerygma and Myth,* www.religion-online.org/showchapter.asp?title=431&C=292.

3. Robert W. Funk, *The Five Gospels* (New York: HarperCollins Publishers, 1993), 2.

4. Some of this information is adapted and condensed from my earlier books, *Choosing Your Faith* (Carol Stream, IL: Tyndale House Publishers, 2008) and *The Questions Christians Hope No One Will Ask* (Carol Stream, IL: Tyndale, 2010), where you can read about this evidence in greater detail.

5. Albert Einstein, *Ideas and Opinions* (New York: Random House, 1994 edition), 43.

6. This argument is classically referred to as the cosmological argument (*kalam* version). For a great discussion on this powerful argument, see William Lane Craig's book *Reasonable Faith*, 3rd ed. (Wheaton, IL: Crossway Books, 2008), chapter 3, especially page 111 and following.

7. Robert Jastrow, *God and the Astronomers*, 2nd ed. (New York: W. W. Norton & Co., 1992), 103 (emphasis mine).

8. Some Christians react negatively to the idea of the Big Bang, but I don't think this is necessary. Biblical theology tells us that God created the universe *ex nihilo*—"out of nothing." That's exactly the kind of event scientists describe as the Big Bang (though many of them try to leave God out of the picture). The evidence points to a cause outside of—and greater than—the universe. This is powerful scientific support for the Bible's teachings!

9. Jastrow, *God and the Astronomers*, 13.

10. Stephen Hawking and Leonard Mlodinow, *The Grand Design* (New York: Bantam Books, 2010), 129.

11. Genesis 1:1

12. Hawking and Mlodinow, *The Grand Design*, 180.

13. Paul Davies, "How Bio-Friendly Is the Universe?" *International Journal of Astrobiology*, vol. 2, no. 2 (2003): 115.

14. Robin Collins, author of a chapter on fine-tuning in *God and Design: The Teleological Argument and Modern Science*, described the situation in Lee Strobel, *The Case for a Creator* (Grand Rapids, MI: Zondervan, 2004), 132:

> When scientists talk about the fine-tuning of the universe, they're generally referring to the extraordinary balancing of the fundamental laws and parameters of physics and the initial conditions of the universe. Our minds can't comprehend the precision of some of them. The result is a universe that has just the right conditions to sustain life. The coincidences are simply too amazing to have been the result of happenstance—as [theoretical physicist, cosmologist, and astrobiologist] Paul Davies said, "the impression of design is overwhelming."

15. From an interview with Dr. Robin Collins in Lee Strobel, *The Case for a Creator* (Grand Rapids, MI: Zondervan, 2004), 132.

16. For recent findings of this kind of evidence, see Paul Davies, *The Goldilocks Enigma: Why Is the Universe Just Right for Life?* (New York: First Mariner Books, 2008).

17. Fred Hoyle, "The Universe: Past and Present Reflections," *Engineering & Science*, November 1981. This can be read at http://calteches.library.caltech.edu/527/2/Hoyle.pdf.

18. As quoted by Robert A. Laidlaw in the original version of *The Reason Why.* See, for example, this edition: (Grand Rapids, MI: Zondervan, 1970), 9–10.

19. Antony Flew and Roy Abraham Varghese, *There Is a God: How the World's Most Notorious Atheist Changed His Mind* (New York: HarperOne, 2007).

20. Lee Strobel and I met and talked extensively with Antony Flew on May 12, 2006, in La Mirada, California. Part

of that conversation was an on-camera interview Strobel conducted with Flew (clips of which can be viewed at www.leestrobel.com).

21. As recorded and discussed in Francis S. Collins's book *The Language of God: A Scientist Presents Evidence for Belief* (New York: Free Press, 2006), 1–3. Also see Stephen C. Meyer's groundbreaking book *Signature in the Cell* (New York: HarperOne, 2009).

22. For an excellent discussion of the moral argument for God's existence, read C. S. Lewis, *Mere Christianity* (New York: HarperOne edition., 2001), 6–7.

23. I delve into these and many other arguments for God's existence and for the truth of Christianity in chapters 9–12 of my book *Choosing Your Faith . . . In a World of Spiritual Options* (Carol Stream, IL: Tyndale House Publishers, 2008).

24. Jean-Paul Sartre, *The Words: The Autobiography of Jean-Paul Sartre*, trans. Bernard Frechtman (New York: Vintage, 1981), 102, 251, 253.

25. Aldous Huxley, *Ends and Means* (London: Chatto & Windus, 1969 edition), 270, 273.

26. In an article titled "Nothing Sacred: Journalist and Provocateur Christopher Hitchens Picks a Fight with God" by Andre Mayer, May 14, 2007, in CBC (www.cbc.ca/arts/books/nothing_sacred.html).

Can the Bible Be Trusted?

1. A summary of these statistics about the Bible can be viewed at www.biblestudy.org/beginner/why-are-there-so-many-bibles-in-the-world.html. Also see: www.economist.com/node/10311317.

2. F. F. Bruce, *The New Testament Documents: Are They Reliable?* 6th ed. (Grand Rapids, MI: Eerdmans, 1981), 11.

3. Sir William M. Ramsay, *The Bearing of Recent Discovery on the Trustworthiness of the New Testament* (London: Hodder

and Stoughton, 1915), 222, as cited in Josh McDowell, *More Than a Carpenter* (Carol Stream, IL: Tyndale House Publishers, 1977), 43–44.

4. Nelson Glueck, *Rivers in the Desert: A History of the Negev* (New York: Farrar, Straus, and Cudahy, 1959), 136.

5. As quoted by Albert Mohler in "The Scandal of Biblical Illiteracy: It's Our Problem," which can be viewed at: www.crosswalk.com/1218766.

6. I love the mix of accuracy and readability in the New Living Translation (NLT), which I am using for most of the biblical quotations in this book. For more information, and to view Scripture portions online, see www.newlivingtranslation.com.

7. As a Christian, I believe it is much more than that. I believe the Bible is the inspired Word of God. But we don't have to start there or ask anyone else to. Also, I'm emphasizing reading the New Testament and especially the four Gospels, but the entire Bible is important and has great value both for our learning and for our lives.

8. For more detailed information on the evidence for the Bible, I recommend Lee Strobel's classic book *The Case for Christ: A Journalist's Personal Investigation of the Evidence for Jesus* (Grand Rapids, MI: Zondervan, 1998).

Are We Accountable to God?

1. See Leviticus 11:44-45; 19:2; 20:7 and 1 Peter 1:16.

2. Proverbs 6:16-18; 1 John 2:16-17

3. C. S. Lewis, *Mere Christianity* (New York: HarperOne edition, 2001), 124.

Who Was Jesus and What Was His Purpose?

1. As quoted in Lee Strobel, *The Case for Christ: A Journalist's Personal Investigation of the Evidence for Jesus* (Grand Rapids, MI: Zondervan, 1998), 91.

2. For more information on the evidence for the divinity of Jesus, see *More Than a Carpenter* by Josh and Sean

McDowell (Carol Stream, IL: Tyndale House Publishers, updated ed., 2009). Also, the evidence for the resurrection of Jesus is breathtaking, but goes beyond the scope of this book. For more information, I recommend *The Case for the Resurrection of Jesus* by Gary R. Habermas and Michael Licona (Grand Rapids, MI: Kregel Publications, 2004).

Is Divine Forgiveness Available?

1. The topic we're discussing here is referred to by theologians as the *Atonement*—and they sometimes debate its core meaning. I believe the Bible makes it clear that the central idea of the Atonement is that Christ came to die for us as our *substitute*, paying the penalty we owed for our sins through his death on the cross. That said, there are many other applications of the atonement of Christ. He was, for example, our victor who triumphed over sin and Satan, but this could only be true if he paid God's just penalty for sin by dying on the cross. All legitimate theories of the Atonement rely upon the foundational biblical teaching of the *substitutionary Atonement*.

2. 1 John 2:2 says, "He himself is the sacrifice that atones for our sins—and not only our sins but the sins of all the world."

3. Emphasis mine.

4. First Peter 1:19-20 reinforces this understanding: "It was the precious blood of Christ, the sinless, spotless Lamb of God. God chose him as your ransom long before the world began, but he has now revealed him to you in these last days."

5. Hugh Ross, *Why the Universe Is the Way It Is* (Grand Rapids, MI: Baker Books, 2008), 31.

6. As reported in *The Harvard Crimson*, "More Stars Found in Universe," which can be seen at www.thecrimson.com/article/2010/12/3/stars-red-galaxies-dwarfs.

7. Candace Adams, "Leading Nanoscientist Builds Big Faith," *Baptist Standard* (March 15, 2002). This can be

viewed at www.baptiststandard.com/2000/3_15/pages/nano.html. Dr. Tour is professor of chemistry, computer science, and mechanical engineering and materials science at Rice University—so apparently he is no "rookie" when it comes to science!

8. For much more on the topic of faith and how to wisely decide what to believe, see my book *Choosing Your Faith . . . In a World of Spiritual Options* (Carol Stream, IL: Tyndale House Publishers, 2008).

9. This teaching is further reinforced in Hebrews 9:22, where it says, "Without the shedding of blood, there is no forgiveness."

What Do I Need to Do?

1. See, for example, www.unclaimed.org/what.

2. The "Do vs. Done" illustration is presented in detail in the book I coauthored with Bill Hybels, *Becoming a Contagious Christian* (Grand Rapids, MI: Zondervan, 1994), and the training course by the same name (coauthored with Lee Strobel and Bill Hybels), updated edition (Grand Rapids, MI: Zondervan, 2007).

3. Emphasis mine.

4. Later in college I did face some doubts and questions about my faith, which I mentioned at the beginning of the book, but those were fairly quickly eradicated as I studied the information and evidence more deeply for myself.